D1451627

on display

on display

DISPLAYING YOUR TREASURES WITH STYLE

RYLAND
PETERS
& SMALL
LONDON NEW YORK

LESLEY DILCOCK

photography by
CATHERINE GRATWICKE

Designer Catherine Randy
Commissioning editor Annabel Morgan
Location research manager Kate Brunt
Location researcher Sarah Hepworth
Production Patricia Harrington
Art director Gabriella Le Grazie
Publishing director Alison Starling

First published in the USA in 2002
by Ryland Peters & Small
519 Broadway
5th Floor
New York, NY 10012
www.rylandpeters.com

10 9 8 7 6 5 4 3 2 1

Libray of Congress Cataloging-in-Publication Data
Dilcock, Lesley.
   On display: displaying your treasures w/style [with style]
/ by Lesley Dilcock
      p. cm
   ISBN 1-84172-274-X
   1. Collectibles in interior decoration. 2. Display of
collectibles. 1. Title

   NK2115.5.C58 D55 2002
   747'.9--dc21

2001048830

Printed and bound in China

To Mum, who hates
clutter, and Dad,
who can't leave
a surface bare.

contents

As a little girl, I collected a menagerie of glass and ceramic animals. Many happy hours were devoted to endlessly rearranging my treasures. Dusting was a terrible trial that resulted in innumerable casualties—a broken leg, a chipped nose. Had it been safely displayed behind glass, my collection might have survived the attentions of my inquisitive baby sister, but, alas, this was not the case!

In those pre-yard sale days, I accompanied my father to auctions and flea markets, antique and junk shops, acquiring along the way a wealth of treasures that I still hold dear today. My student garret heaved with a steadily increasing number of prized possessions, the most obscure of which was a moth-eaten stuffed alligator. I enjoyed playing around with colors and shapes to create still lives that occupied every available surface.

Nowadays, my house is something akin to a living museum, a celebration of the many things from all eras and continents that I find aesthetically pleasing. It's certainly no minimalist domain, although I do admire the discipline that reigns in some homes. Mine is an irreverent mix, but it makes for an interesting enviroment to live in, and there's plenty of mileage for rearranging to my heart's content.

In my work as an interiors stylist, I do exactly the same thing, but generally using borrowed objects. Sometimes I attempt to "style" other people's homes, displaying the items they possess to their best advantage. I hope this book will help you realize the possibilities of your own treasures, and that my suggestions for showing them off will provide you with all the inspiration and ideas you need to create your own wonderful displays.

introduction

PICTURE THIS   An eye-catching vintage scarf, made into a striking scatter cushion, together with a painting inspired by the same print, are dramatically showcased in an all-white room (opposite page). The combination of picture and painting is spiced up by the off-center positioning of the cushion, which creates a more dynamic visual effect. Displays do not always have to be on a grand scale. Pay attention to the little details in your home—such as these mirrored picture frames, embroidered table linen, and *trompe l'oeil* effects—and you will invest it with an indefinable character and individuality (below left, center, and right).

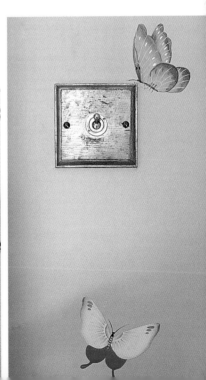

what to
display

what to display

Although the very word "display" may bring to mind your grandmother's collection of china figurines or the fanciful realms of window dressing, this book takes a very different approach. In it, I hope to encourage your freedom of expression and your confidence in your own taste, and help you to reconsider what exactly is "worthy" of being on display.

Before we address the question of how to display your treasures, let's first consider what you might want to display. What moves you, appeals to you, speaks to you, seduces you? Is it a few well-loved childhood relics or a recent impulse buy? A fabulous piece of fabric brought back from a trip abroad or a postcard from friends? An antique vase handed down through the generations or a handful of shells or leaves discovered on the beach or in the local park? A piece of scrap metal retrieved from a dumpster or an outrageously expensive must-have bought at an auction? It may be any or all of those things, and, believe it or not, they can all make wonderful displays.

Recognizing the potential of your possessions is the first step to displaying them successfully. Take a new

WHATEVER TAKES YOUR FANCY This exuberant painting of parrots, hung in the artist's New York loft (opposite page, left), provides a backdrop for the wealth of glass on display. Color-coordinated glass groupings recur throughout the space. A blank wall is brought to life (opposite page, right) by a linear display of pieces of gold embossed Chinese papers that catch the light and set the wall aglow. The owner of another New York loft (right) is a collector of quirky "paint-by-numbers" art: the pictures are displayed in random formation on the bathroom wall. The colors of these plastic and bakelite bowls and napkin rings (below and below right) endeared them to their illustrator owner, who displays them casually in her kitchen.

A TASTE FOR PATTERN Boldly patterned tiles perfectly complement a coordinating collection of decorative blue-and-white ceramics in a London kitchen (left). In the same home, an impressive collection of decorative powder compacts is proudly displayed in the living room (opposite page). Set on each side of the sofa are occasional tables with glass tops that contain an array of delicate treasures, including this fine collection of exquisite compacts that date back to the 1940s and 1950s. The designer collector of these compacts has a passion for the glamour and sophistication of this period, and has amassed an eclectic collection of feminine accessories and quirky novelty items that date back to her favorite era.

ON THE SHELF The display unit can house prized possessions in great style. This architect's apartment in New York (left), has a custom-designed teak unit that holds African artefacts of all shapes and sizes. Meanwhile, a renowned New York ceramicist leaves no shelf, however narrow, bare of his designs (below). Even the much-maligned radiator can prove additional display space (opposite page, left). An Oriental theme pervades this Paris apartment, with fans and a china doll complementing the paper and bamboo standard lamp. Little lead figures, the only survivors of a long-lost farmyard of animals, provide an amusing diversion atop a narrow frame (opposite page, right). They inhabit a world of preposterous proportions, the giant chicken contentedly following the farmer's wife like a pet puppy.

look at the things you own. When you open a drawer in search of a pair of socks or the backdoor key and you catch a glimpse of an old photo that makes you smile, bring it out and prop it on the mantelpiece or pin it to the wall—it will make you smile every time you pass. A favorite piece of packaging from a product that has been discontinued might still hold a place in your heart, so retrieve it from the wastebasket—after all, you wouldn't dream of discarding a book so indiscriminately once it has been read.

You could allow your passion for flowers to come in from the garden and blossom into a display of floral ceramics. A love of machinery might lead you on a journey to industrial reclamation or salvage merchants in search of the abstract shapes you want on your walls. Either a chance find or a carefully considered investment could be the starting point for a dazzling

display. Perhaps an unexpected gift will be the start of an obsession, sparking a lifelong hunt for more of the same. Those bits and pieces once bought on impulse in a foreign market, but which have never left their boxes, should be reconsidered, and even your more obvious display pieces—glass, ceramics, or pictures—could probably be combined in more exciting ways.

The secret of a successful display is to allow your personality free reign. Exhibit items that are dear to your heart—old postcards, empty perfume bottles, or costume jewelry. You'll be surprised at how old and new, big and small, patterned and plain can sit together quite happily. The most obscure and unexpected items can have real presence *en masse*. And the best thing is that when creating a display, your aim is to please yourself—the decisions are all yours, and you are answerable to no one else.

TAKE A CLOSER LOOK If you think you are short of display space, look again. Even an unprepossessing concrete ledge can offer a home to a collection of tiny treasures, as demonstrated here by this exhibition of dozens of slender wood segments in a New York interior (above left). Some items on display always receive a second look. A wine lover was the recipient of this painstaking collage of hundreds of discarded wine-bottle corks (above right). The unusual creation is now on permanent display in his study, and is guaranteed to bring back happy memories of convivial evenings sharing a good bottle of wine with friends.

A FEAST FOR THE EYES A narrow shelf or a side table offers a multitude of display possibilities, as do a group of empty glass vases. Here, a collection of simple glass flower vases have been filled with a number of contrasting textures to create a pleasing tableau. The contents—from string to crystals, buttons to feathers—are linked by their soft, neutral tones to create a restful and harmonious composition in a quiet corner of the kitchen (right). A fine set of antique cameos, with their subtle tints and delicate reliefs, forms a display of miniature works of art that invite hours of quiet appreciation and contemplation (below).

EXHIBIT ITEMS THAT ARE DEAR TO YOUR HEART— OLD POSTCARDS, EMPTY PERFUME BOTTLES OR COSTUME JEWELRY. YOU'LL BE SURPRISED AT HOW OLD AND NEW, BIG AND SMALL, PATTERNED AND PLAIN CAN SIT TOGETHER QUITE HAPPILY.

From hats to shoes, underwear to overcoats, homespun to *haute couture*, there's a wealth of fabulous fashion paraphernalia to put on show. Collectible couture is an expensive business. Valuable, of great beauty and historical significance, and often extremely fragile, many couture items have to be kept behind closed doors, cocooned in tissue and stored in surroundings that are heat controlled and light deprived. More relaxed fun can be had with decorative fashion items that are not quite so precious or revered.

A gloriously girly dress that is just too pretty to be hidden away could hang on the closet door. A fragile Victorian lace blouse, light as a feather, might be suspended from an elaborate frame. Hang transparent

fashion and accessories

THE FEMININE TOUCH This fragile Oriental jacket (opposite page) is a treasured flea-market find. Beloved for its pattern and coloring, it has found a permanent home hanging from an armoire door in a London bedroom. A unique handbag (below left) takes pride of place atop an equally individual chair covered in elaborate satin fabric, while the sensuous lines of a glass dish show off a jumble of new and vintage fabric flower corsages in a designer's boudoir (below right). Pretty shoes deserve to be shown off rather than hidden from view (above right).

AN ASSORTMENT OF ACCESSORIES A vintage satin nightdress adorns an armoire door painted in a similarly gentle hue (left). Pretty as a picture, a colorful cluster of posy bags perfectly complements the chinoiserie-style floral wallpaper in the hall of a London designer's home (below left). In a London illustrator's home, a love of red shoes is evident in this display of old and current favorites in a shelved alcove (below right), reflecting the fantasy of every little girl who coveted Dorothy's glittery red shoes in *The Wizard of Oz*. Bejeweled mules stand on tiptoe on a windowsill (opposite page, right). The same window is home to an assortment of chain belts and an ever-changing array of dainty handbags (opposite page, left).

MAKE SHOES A DECORATIVE FEATURE IN THE BEDROOM OR HALL, LINING UP YOUR FAVORITES ALONG A WALL, UP THE STAIRS, AND ON THE WINDOWSILL, OR ARRANGE THEM ON PURPOSE-BUILT SHELVING.

slip dresses from the curtain rod, the better to appreciate their gossamer sheerness. A patterned jacket would make a lively display against clashing wallpaper.

Old shoes with holes worn in their soles may capture your romantic imagination, but so, too, might this season's latest styles. Make shoes a decorative feature in the bedroom or hall, lining up your favorites along a wall, up the stairs, and on the windowsill, or arrange them on purpose-built shelving.

A collection of hats possesses endless display possibilities. Arrange them on a wall, hang them from a row of pegs, or pile them high on top of armoires and chests. You could observe a restricted color palette for a more disciplined display, or collect hats of all shapes and sizes, and enjoy their variety and contrast. Fashioned from a huge variety of materials—felt, fur, feathers, straw, or leather—hats range from the austere to the fanciful. More restrained styles include the

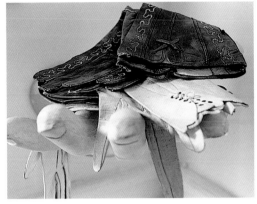

SOFT AND SERENE OR FAB AND FUNKY?

The scene is set for a modern boudoir with clean lines and delicate, cool colors (opposite page). A feminine touch is added in the shape of a floaty lace top that swings from the edge of a kitsch 1960s print. Toiletries in pretty packaging are neatly arrayed upon a small tray to continue the uncluttered, pared-down effect. The same London home vibrates with color and pattern in the hall (left). Fashion accessories have been made from groovy upholstery fabrics that date back to the 1960s and '70s. The molded plastic and aluminum chair adds to the period feel, and the vase of coral-pink gladioli reinforces the vibrant color palette. A giant plaster hand (above) reaches out from the wall to provide a particularly suitable home for a collection of vintage leather gloves.

BEST FOOT FORWARD If your passion for shoes borders on obsession, it's likely that your collection of fantasy footwear will demand plenty of storage space. After all, you can only wear one pair at a time! As might be guessed, the owner of this shoe collection (above) has a personal involvement with the design and production of clogs. Her storage solution is this wall in her hall, which has been covered with narrow shelves and devoted to an impressive display of striped and multicolored examples.

masculine fedora, trilby, bowler, or top hat, while frivolous and flirty concoctions of net, straw, and feathers are too appealing to be hidden away in boxes.

Similarly, shawls that are far too pretty to be folded away in drawers can be draped over chairs, tables, and sofas. Alternatively, they can be pressed into service as unusual window coverings or framed and hung like pictures, so their patterns, embroidery, and trailing fringes can be appreciated anew every day. Silk scarves with decorative designs can also be framed or given a new lease on life as throw-pillow covers.

Children's clothes are endlessly appealing. The small scale and the feelings of nostalgia they evoke make them a popular choice for collectors. My first pair of red galoshes, dating back to the 1950s, are proudly displayed on my bedroom shelf. A delicate frieze of intricate lace and embroidered cotton baby nightgowns hangs around my bathroom walls. I have a passion for something even more miniature—dolls' clothes. Tiny crocheted shifts and impossibly small hand-knitted cardigans, complete with weeny pearl buttons, are framed and on display in many of my rooms.

SHAWLS THAT ARE TOO PRETTY TO BE FOLDED AWAY IN DRAWERS CAN BE DRAPED OVER CHAIRS, TABLES, AND SOFAS, OR PRESSED INTO SERVICE AS UNUSUAL WINDOW COVERINGS.

EYE-CATCHING EFFECTS The more decorative the accessory, the more likely you are to want to keep it on show. Finding places around the home where your possessions will give you pleasure without becoming a hindrance is a challenge. Experiment with empty ledges, like the footrests of these stools, which play host to colorful velvet slippers (above left). Bags can hang from doorknobs (above center) while belts and jewelry look wonderful draped casually over chair backs or bedsteads (above right).

ALL THAT GLITTERS An antique dressmaker's dummy, now devoid of its stand and with its fabric worn away to reveal a sensuous décolletage, is just the place to show off delicate trinkets.

FINISHING TOUCHES A carved wooden headboard is home to a collection of rosaries in this London bedroom (right). This collection of 1960s rings, worn only occasionally, nestle in the hollow of a modern ceramic dish commandeered for the dual job of storage and display (below right). Meanwhile, a cluster of colorful floral brooches have emerged from the jewelry box and landed like butterflies on this blank canvas (below left).

jewelry

Mirroring the rollercoaster ride that is the history of fashion, costume and junk jewelry offers a cornucopia of display possibilities. Often I'm enchanted by a piece of jewelry and can't resist buying it, even though I have no intention of ever wearing it. But that's fine, because costume jewelry—whether it is made from paste, glass, semiprecious stones, rhinestones, wood, or plastic—makes for wonderful displays.

Necklaces, strings of beads, and chains are easy to find homes for—hang them from any hook or handle, or drape them over headboards or the corner of a mirror. Bangles can be balanced and stacked on any surface, slotted or strung together, or heaped in deep bowls and shallow dishes.

Brooches have been exiled in the fashion wilderness for some time now, but often they are charming miniature works of art. A collection of antique cameos could be individually framed and hung together like a group of portraits. Pin a cluster of floral ceramic brooches on a fabric wall hanging or even your curtains. The fabric corsage, much favored in the 1940s, has been enjoying a massive resurgence in fashion of late. Vintage silk and satin confections are sometimes crumpled and faded but are no less beautiful. Modern versions are fun and feisty in vibrant, vivid colors. Keep them on show as you

would real flowers, in a pretty shallow vase or bowl, or make a garland from them to drape around a mirror or your headboard.

Dresser sets designed specifically to display and hold jewelry were once very popular—the ceramic hand to hold rings and the china stand with a perforated top intended for hat pins are two I particularly remember from my childhood. Look out for them on visits to secondhand stores or yard sales, and give them the chance to return to the task they were designed for.

Ex-display stands from jewelers or milliners will also provide the perfect showcase for your jewelry. For a more whimsical touch, invest in a plaster bust, be it Mozart or Madonna, and bedeck it with your costume jewelry, complete with tiara. Alternatively, a disparate collection of colorful jewelry could be best appreciated in a see-through container—a plexiglass box, a glass storage jar, or a clear vase.

UNEXPECTED ADORNMENTS Integrate favorite pieces of jewelry into your home so they become part of the decor. Strings of round red beads bring a vivid flash of color to the bedroom door in this Paris apartment (opposite page, left). Different textures are highlighted when engraved metal bangles are placed upon a rusted surface (opposite page, above right). The simple forms of these primitive African ladders are best appreciated when they are displayed against a smooth white wall. One is decorated with a handful of tribal beads (opposite page, below right). A trio of diminutive wooden display dummies (right) is the ideal means of showcasing or even storing unusual necklaces and bracelets, and is guaranteed to draw the eye upon a dressing table or mantelpiece in the bedroom.

COMING UP ROSES Vintage headscarves are just too entrancing to be incarcerated in a drawer. Choose a selection that is unified by similar colors or decorative themes, and they can be made into an eye-catching set of pillow covers, guaranteed to enliven a room (opposite page and below left). The now almost defunct pocket handkerchief once enjoyed a colorful past, as is evident in this ingenious display (below right). The folded handkerchiefs are draped over a miniature ladder propped on a radiator.

textiles

Textiles, from household linens such as dishtowels to intricate works of art such as tapestries, are a constant source of delight. Stack beloved pieces on open shelves so you can touch and see your treasures on a regular basis. Even the most fragile piece of cloth can be preserved for your delectation by framing and hanging it well away from the sun's destructive rays.

Imaginative thinking can give pieces a new lease on life, so they play both a functional and a decorative role in your home. When hung at the window, a lace shawl is instantly transformed into the prettiest and daintiest of curtains. A collection of silk scarves can be recycled into mouthwatering pillow covers, while old jackets can be transformed into delightful chairback covers, and a tablecloth with exquisite embroidery will conceal the drabbest sofa. Collect scraps of treasured fabrics so they can be turned into patchwork and given a new lease on life as a bedspread or throw. Exotic travels are another good opportunity to amass unusual decorative textiles to display in the home.

LIFE'S RICH TAPESTRY Traditionally, the thick stone walls of grand buildings were lined with tapestries, to provide insulation from the cold as well as for decorative effect. Nowadays, any textiles, from sheer silk shawls to hand-woven carpets, can imitate this effect. In a London designer's home (opposite page), an exquisite embroidered panel sits behind a sofa adorned with pillows and throws covered in coordinated fabrics. At the other end of the room, small fragments of textiles are framed and sit companionably together on the mantelpiece (left). Snuggly comforters covered in dainty floral prints are too delicious to sit in the blanket box awaiting a cold snap. Drape them over the ends of the bed to create softly padded head- and foot-rests (below).

Many people collect everyday items or are attracted to objects with a former working life. Old keys are one good example. Separated from their matching locks, they may seem candidates for the scrap heap, but in fact they can captivate with their suggestion of untold secrets or wrongful incarceration. Some examples are ornate and imposing in size, but the smaller, simpler styles are easier to come by, and are equally beguiling.

All manner of tools from the carpenter's workshop can prove worthy of display. When no longer in use, old planes and pliers or saws and squares become purely pleasing forms and shapes. Equally, the dressmaker's atelier provides a wealth of attractive sewing regalia, from ribbonlike measuring tapes to the impressive proportions of tailor's shears. Old horticultural implements, with their countryside connotations, bring to mind rural idylls and a bygone age. Even the most urban of settings can enjoy the rustic images that they conjure up.

If its size, shape, or form pleases you, nothing is too disreputable or dilapidated to be displayed. Ex-industrial appliances and parts, such as presses and molds, are interesting in their own right. So, too, are the inner workings of massive machinery. Immense metal washers or cogs become abstract patterns when liberated from the factory floor, and can make for a very contemporary presentation.

Don't make the mistake of thinking that everyday items are too mundane to be displayed. Scissors, corkscrews, and bottle openers may sound like unlikely candidates for exhibition, but they all have design variations that can lead to an intriguing display.

tools and implements

RECYCLING A New York sculptress finds salvaged industrial items inspiring, so much so that she uses them to decorate her home as well as featuring them in her creations. Here, a collection of over-sized metal washers form a constellation on the wall, while an old press carries an intriguing umbrella carcass, part of a work in progress (above). In another part of her living space, a skeletonlike structure is suspended from the ceiling (opposite page). A closer look reveals that it is assembled from pickax heads and handles. The wall-mounted wooden molds for machinery parts continue the industrial theme.

ON FORM (OVERLEAF) While the components are individually of little importance, a display of numerous small keys proves an intriguing sight above the bed in a London home (above left). In the dressing room, the same color scheme offers a restrained backdrop for a set of tailor's shears and large scissors (below left). On a Paris balcony, an amusing visual pun presents itself in the shape of a bunch of watering-can roses grouped in a florallike arrangement (center). An old ladder finds itself supporting many tape measures of varying vintage that have been casually draped over the rungs and left to unwind in curls and corkscrews (right).

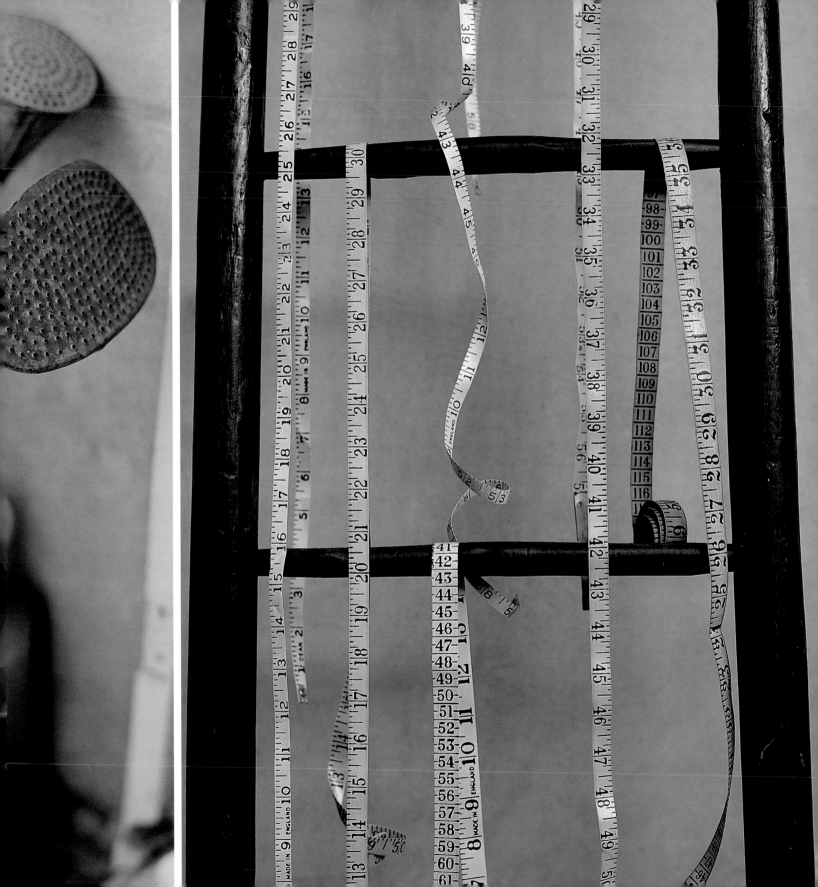

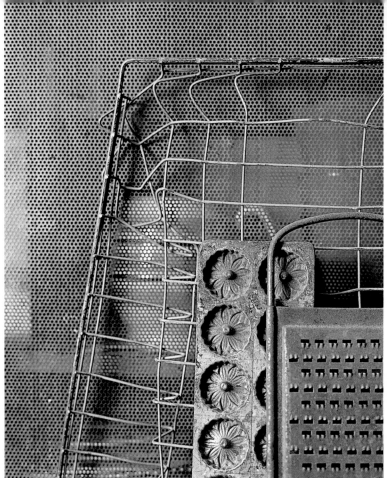

kitchenware

Throughout history, the culinary world has provided us with an enormous range of implements designed especially for cooking and eating. Over the years, technological developments and changing eating habits have rendered many of them redundant, but the patina of age these implements have developed and the nostalgia they evoke has resulted in the avid accumulation of all types of kitchenware.

Many simple, functional utensils possess bold and graphic shapes and forms that are enormously appealing. Wire cooling racks, with their metal grid formation, the perforated spherical bowls of shiny stainless steel colanders, even the humble metal or wooden spoon, with its sensuous, undulating curves—these items can seduce the eyes of even the most dedicated minimalist.

One perfect example is the food mold. The simplest of outer shells conceals an inner inverted image of intricate curves and contours. They range from china pudding molds in ironstone, creamware, and drabware to tin-lined copper molds used for mousses and aspics. Newer enamel or glass versions conceal their shapes less secretively, but remain intriguing and are relatively inexpensive. On a smaller scale, metal chocolate molds, with their detailed designs of flora and fauna, are particularly charming.

MANY SIMPLE UTENSILS POSSESS GRAPHIC SHAPES AND FORMS THAT ARE HUGELY APPEALING. EVEN THE HUMBLE SPOON, WITH ITS SENSUOUS, UNDULATING CURVES, CAN PROVE CURIOUSLY SEDUCTIVE.

CULINARY COLLECTIONS Kitchen paraphernalia tends to be functional, but it also possesses great potential for decorative display. In this London home (opposite page, left and right, and right), subdued tones prevail. The old glass jars and bottles, in assorted shapes and sizes, have a green cast that complements the battered meat locker they sit on, which is used to store dishes. A set of greenish-gray dotted plates have been arranged on the wall nearby. Into this arrangement are introduced the shapes and textures of various rusty metal molds, graters, and wire cooling racks. Even a squashed office filing tray, found flattened in the street, has won a place in the display, owing to its coordinating color and shape. The same kitchen is home to a set of pleasingly rustic spotted French china (opposite page, below left). It was collected over the years on ski trips in the French Alps and now sits in a dot-to-dot display in the same kitchen, echoing the pattern of the dotted plates on the walls.

Cooking pots, dishes, flatware, and kitchen utensils from far-flung lands are fascinating. Chopsticks, with their accompanying ceramic rests, are inexpensive, easily obtainable, and very decorative. Also appealing is Oriental kitchenware fashioned from bamboo, such as steamers that can be stacked several storys high.

With the development of plastic during the twentieth century, a new range of kitchen accessories appeared. The hygienic, easy-care properties of this exciting new material, together with its ease of mass production, resulted in affordable, colorful, and often kitsch designs appearing in millions of households. Low cost, however, meant that these items were not valued and were often thrown away. Now, in the early stages of a new millennium, an appreciation and awareness of such items is blossoming, to such an extent that the price of collectibles from the culinary kingdom may follow those from the couture firmament and rise sky-high. There is, nevertheless, still the chance of spotting bargain buys at yard sales, in thrift stores, and antique fairs, so if bakelite bowls or soda siphons tempt you, snap them up before it's too late.

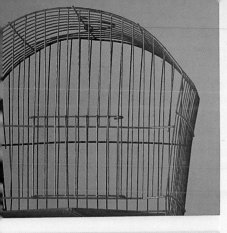

WORTH A SECOND LOOK The benefits of open shelving in a kitchen are those of convenience and practicality (this page). They also offer an added bonus—an opportunity to put on show the things that please in an orderly and attractive fashion. Here, the mix is diverse—stylishly packaged food is balanced by a stack of table linen, and a birdcage and cricket ball add a quirky splash of red to the neutral tones. These French enamel strainers (opposite page), in subtle shades, possess an allure that has resulted in their display on a kitchen cupboard.

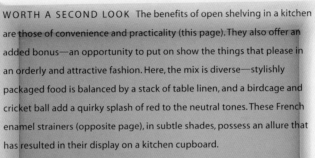

SOPHISTICATED SHADES Color-coordinated displays are invariably a success, as a variety of different shapes and designs will sit happily together if they share a section of the color spectrum. The muted, sludgy shades and curvaceous forms of these ceramic vessels (left) make for a pleasing display in the home of a distinguished New York ceramicist. Each has a slightly differing naturalistic shape and varied relief patterns. The pieces are informally arranged, but the harmonious color scheme lends the display a sense of coherence and prevents it from looking random or cluttered.

ceramics

They crack, they chip, and they smash; yet despite the fragility of ceramics, countless pieces have endured thousands of years. Ceramics span countries and centuries, and come in a multitude of shapes and forms, from the simplistic to the ornate, the functional to the decorative, the plain to the patterned, the shiny to the matt, the heavy to the delicate, and the priceless to those picked up for just a few cents—something for everyone, in short.

The Modernist designs that came out of Scandinavia in the middle of the twentieth century are particularly popular nowadays because their simple forms and forward-looking designs touch a chord with contemporary taste. Postwar Poole pottery is a British classic that has recently found itself a new audience. Other darlings of the contemporary home include hand-crafted or hand-thrown pieces, owing to a renewed appreciation of the potter's craft and the fascination for all things simple and Orient-inspired. Even mass-produced modern ceramics play an important part in the latest interior trends.

SHELF MATES In a New York loft, a designer has amassed a collection of vintage oven-to-tableware that shares simple lines and off-beat colors (left and opposite page, below left). The area in which this collection is displayed combines custom-built modern shelving fitted around an original pillar—a reminder of the loft's previous existence as a warehouse. The scuffed and distressed surface of the pillar contrasts with the sleek lines and glossy finish of the ceramics. In a simpler arrangement that is no less effective (below), three Australian bowls sit neatly in line along a pickled wooden bench.

A TASTE OF THE TRADITIONAL

Don't dismiss conventional display techniques as dull or boring. Displaying plates on walls is an age-old method of showing off your favorite china. This Paris apartment (left) is crammed with the most bizarre and bohemian of pieces, but in one corner, a sense of calmness reigns. The wall is home to a display of serving platters. Cracked and chipped with age and use, they sit beside a matching pair of busts. The whole arrangement is unified by the rich and creamy colors. A London designer collects only the prettiest and most delicately patterned bone china teacups and saucers (opposite page). The black lacquer table they sit upon reflects their dainty shapes and patterns in its glossy depths.

IN CONTRAST These shelf companions have been placed together to create an eloquent
study of simple forms within a restricted color range. The lower shelf holds mugs for everyday
use, while the upper shelf holds a selection of pieces that are intended to be purely decorative.

When collecting ceramics, should you limit yourself to a particular color or style, a period of history, or even a specific factory? For a serious collector or for a completely coherent display, restrictions are essential, but ultimately what you put on show comes down to personal preference. Thematic groupings can be great fun. Choose figurines and create a crowd of extras on a cinematic scale. Perhaps dainty floral teacups and saucers could crowd your shelves. Maybe leaf patterns, from a Minton majolica foliage dish to a Carlton Ware waterlily plate, could ramble over your walls in abundance. Blue-and-white striped or willow-patterned pottery might capture your heart, as it has thousands of others' and lead to a whole interior being devoted solely to that color combination.

With such great diversity of shape, color, design, and cost on offer, it would be easy to imagine that a collection of ceramics would be subject to snobbery and prejudices. Happily, this is not the case these days. You may be the proud possessor of a priceless Ming vase or an avid collector of Victorian souvenir china. Your tastes dictate your choices, and they are all your own—long may they remain so.

HARMONIOUS HUES Neutral shades of off-white unify a collection of kitchen ceramics on open shelves (above). A glazed hand, dating from the 1950s, sits in front of a contemporary plate to constitute an effective still life within a larger arrangement (far left). Gelatin molds are much sought by collectors of kitchen ceramics. Here, they are stacked informally (left).

mirrors, pictures, and frames

GALLERY LIVING In downtown Manhattan, an architect-designed loft is the domestic setting for a collection of contemporary art. The loft's inhabitants are gallery owners, and their home functions as an extension of their business. The living area is also an exhibition space, with photographic art hung in a grid formation along one wall (opposite page). In a hall (above right), a shallow shelf allows several artworks to be shown in a flexible display that is ever-changing. Itself an artwork, this mirror reflects the two different display techniques—the symmetrical arrangement of frames of a uniform size and shape, and the more informal assemblage of pictures of varied size and style (above). The mirror effectively appears to be a window to another room and adds vibrancy owing to the reflected light it throws into the space.

In my opinion, mirrors are magical. They reflect images and refract light with the most bewitching and beguiling effects. A room without a mirror is somehow a room without a soul. Bring several of them into a room and you will immediately introduce a kaleidoscope of light and color into the space.

Interior designers often use mirrors to alter our perceptions of light and space—how often have you almost walked into a mirrored wall only to realize it's a cunning illusion? Well-placed mirrors can add a sense of space and light to even the smallest and darkest rooms. A narrow, dark hall will be dramatically illuminated when hung with mirrors of varying sizes and shapes. Each one might be an inexpensive thrift-store find, picked up for next to nothing, but the overall effect is a dramatic one.

THE IMAGES YOU PUT ON DISPLAY IN YOUR HOME OFFER AN INSIGHT INTO
YOUR PERSONALITY, ALTERING OR CONFIRMING A VISITOR'S OPINION OF YOU.

Looking glasses come in myriad shapes and sizes. Some are resplendent with elaborate and ornate mounts, others fish-eyed or beveled. Some are so old that the backing is rubbed away and the silvering is tarnished and faded. Old mirrors can be resilvered if they do not reflect clearly, but mottled and cloudy glass is atmospheric and possesses its own charm. Choose whatever suits your mood and money, but make sure every room holds at least one mirror.

The images you choose to put on display in your home offer a insight into your personality, perhaps altering or confirming a visitor's opinion of you. Investment in art is an exclusive and expensive

business at the highest levels, but original paintings and photographs can also be bought at end-of-year college shows or small-scale exhibitions and auctions. You might be lucky enough to find a picture or print that appeals to you in a flea market or yard sale.

A wide range of images are worthy of display. Perhaps postcards are your thing, in which case you could create a miniature gallery on your mantelpiece— a collection of images to add to or discard at will. Find interesting places to display favorite images—cover a door with postcards or decorate the fridge with family photographs. Pin or tape particular favorites to the wall to create a collage that's reminiscent of teenage

FRAMED Once framed, a picture or object seems to gain more significance or importance. Here (opposite page, right), a button-lover has cards and jars full of her favorites on show, but her cherished mother-of-pearl buttons have been singled out for further attention. The old frames add character to the grouping. In the same London home (opposite page, left), the hall is enlivened with an extensive collection of mirrors. None of them is a particularly expensive or precious piece, but the overall visual effect is rather dramatic and brings light and interest to an uninspiring passageway.

SHELVED In a New York loft, contemporary metal shelving holds both modern Japanese ceramics and a group of treasured family photographs in very traditional frames, the visual link being faces (left). In another Manhattan home, a large empty frame forms the backbone of a considered still life (above). The combination of frame, bowl, and African sculpture is an unconventional one, but the composition is entirely successful—balanced in shape, size, and color.

years, when plastering pictures of rock stars around your bedroom was second nature. A display of postcards could take the place of tiles in a kitchen or bathroom. Position a collage of images above a sink or a stove and then cover the wall with glass.

Once framed, an image seems to take on an air of consequence. Each era has its own style of frame, ranging from the extravagances of the baroque to functional 1930s bakelite examples. Modern frames are every bit as varied as antique specimens. A picture can be greatly enhanced by the addition of an unexpected frame. When you place an abstract modern image in an extravagantly detailed gilt frame, the contrast is often surprisingly successful. Equally, a more traditional painting, when relieved of its heavy frame, can be seen with new eyes. Often you might be unable to resist a

THE MORE THE MERRIER A prolific New York artist utilizes the vast wall spaces in his large loft to create a personal gallery of his work. Each room offers a different, vibrantly colored backdrop. In the yellow room (opposite page), the paintings vary in size and style of frame, but a religious theme prevails. The display has evolved slowly over the years, giving it a random, unstructured look. Pictures hang alongside each other higgledy piggledy and even spill on to the sofa. In the blue bedroom (above left), small but colorful images in dramatic frames crowd the walls. A change of scale is employed at the end of the long hall (above right), where a single large canvas fills most of the available wall space. On the sideboard below, framed family photographs are displayed.

YOU'RE ON CAMERA Having fun with photos means leaving conventional arrangements behind. In this London home (right), the fridge has been transformed from a functional appliance into an eye-catching gallery of family, vacation, and celebratory snapshots. The photographs cover every available inch and guarantee a smile every time the owner reaches for a glass of milk. A favorite photo deserves special treatment. Developments in photographic printing now make it possible to blow up images to dramatic dimensions. Here, a vacation shot has been enlarged to life-size, the better to appreciate its architectural and textural interest (opposite page).

frame, even if you have no image in mind for it. Some frames are so pleasing in their own right that you may choose to display them empty.

Grouped images, framed or otherwise, always have more impact. Arrange similarly sized pictures in a neat grid or go crazy and cover the whole wall. Don't be inhibited by color—anything too tasteful is the equivalent of background muzak. A narrow shelf or ledge is the ideal exhibition space for a continually changing array of images. This works particularly well in a long hall, creating a gallery effect. When propped rather than hung, pictures are far easier to change on a whim and offer more spontaneity when it comes to display. Different-colored and -sized frames will keep the overall look loose and casual.

Glass-fronted box frames, which are now available in many chain stores, will allow you much more diversity in your displays. The depth of the frame allows you to frame a variety of objects, from a pair of baby shoes to a handful of appealing pebbles.

glassware

Glass is a remarkable man-made invention. Its basic ingredients of sand and soda are a humble and unlikely starting point for the alchemical process that has produced such wonders for over 6,000 years. The earliest surviving glass containers are those found in Egypt and Mesopotamia, which date from 1500 B.C.

A punitive tax on weight was imposed on glass between 1745 and 1845, making the heavy lead glass then produced prohibitively expensive. It was the Industrial Revolution and the introduction of mass-production methods that made it affordable and accessible to all for the first time. The result was attractive pressed glass for everyday home use. The pressing techniques gradually improved, and by the 1880s the molds were extremely sophisticated and complex. In fact, glassware reached a peak of popularity during the nineteenth century, when molded glass convincingly imitated handmade and hand-cut polished lead glass.

Glass comes in a huge array of forms, colors, and finishes. Collecting just one particular type or color is a disciplined and focused approach that is guaranteed to result in a very coherent display. Early pressed glass is interesting, since it carries some fantastically intricate patterning in both naturalistic and geometric designs. Some commemorative pieces are particularly charming. Then there's the extraordinary metallic luster of carnival glass, the densely opaque milk glass, slag glass with its swirling, marbled effect, decorated designs with reverse transfer prints, or handpainted patterns,

COLOR AND LIGHT The owner of these pieces (left and above) has a passion for 1960s glassware that would, not so very long ago, have been reviled as the ultimate in bad taste. Nowadays, this display of boldly colored examples occupies pride of place in a stylish London home. The items have been chosen for their strong colors, lines, and patterns. The same reassessment of what's hot and what's not has found a new audience for the charms of the somewhat kitsch glass fish. Here (opposite page, below), in the same London home, a school of colorful examples glides across a tabletop, picking up the colors in the modern artwork behind. In a New York loft, a sunny corner is devoted to the era of shagpile carpets and orange decor (opposite page, above). An original Knoll glass coffee table supports a cluster of glass paperweights— intricate colors captured in a glass bubble.

CONTEMPORARY OR TRADITIONAL? The clean lines of these Italian glass vessels give them a modern edge that suits the simplicity of the space they occupy. The splash of vivid color they produce looks all the more vibrant against the white backdrop (this page). Meanwhile, in another London apartment (opposite page), the mood is more nostalgic. Pressed glass candlesticks are elegant in ones and twos, but a positive triumph *en masse*. This long dining table dances with light even on the darkest days, while at night candles illuminate the space dramatically.

TRY TO POSITION GLASS WITH LIGHT BEHIND OR BELOW THE DISPLAY. YOU WILL BE REWARDED WITH EXQUISITE EFFECTS, AS THE FRAGILE AND TRANSLUCENT QUALITY OF THE MATERIAL IS HIGHLIGHTED.

novelty shapes, or super-sleek designs from Murano, the center of Italian glass. The list goes on and on. Your preference may be for Victorian cranberry glass or the glass produced by the Whitefriars factory in the 1950s. The modern glass industry continues to exploit this wonderful medium, and many contemporary pieces are created purely as display items rather than for functional purposes.

To the food and drink industry, glass is a form of packaging. Long before recycling programs got underway, the glass jar and the milk bottle were frequently reused, owing to inclination rather than conscience. Old glass jars are great containers, ideal for storing and displaying small collectables like beads or

buttons. The humble milk bottle has evolved in shape and capacity over the years. Early wide-necked styles are great receptacles for kitchen utensils or can be utilized as chunky vases. Some soft-drink bottles have become modern icons. Glass food containers, such as jelly jars, can be given a new lease on life as votive-candle holders or miniature hurricane lamps.

If possible, try to position glass with light behind or below the display. You will be rewarded with exquisite effects, as the fragile and translucent quality of the material is highlighted. Play around with mirrored shelves and tables, placing treasured pieces of glass on top to double their impact. Don't leave glass to languish in a dark unlit corner or its delicate beauty will be lost.

LIVING WITH GLASS An impressively
proportioned conservatory that doubles as
an artist's studio (right) is brought alive with
a riotous assembly of opulent glassware. Every
surface is thronged with colorful glass bottles
of undulating and elongated shape and form,
creating a miniature citadel of minarets and
towers. The collection also encompasses an
arresting still life of turquoise glass fruit
resting on a silver dish (below) and a
magnificent display of pressed glass
candlesticks that bring a sense of fairytale
splendor to a dining table (opposite page,
right). Delicate drinking glasses (opposite
page, left) are perfectly at home displayed on
a glass tray and a mirrored surface, which
doubles the effect of the slender lines that
decorate their surfaces.

the natural world

NATURAL BEAUTY A collection of primitive flints and other archeological finds has been wired to an old wooden board and now sits displayed on a low easel in front of a vast cabinet chock-full of other eccentric treasures (opposite page). The whole of this idiosyncratic Paris apartment is crammed with the bizarre and the beautiful. Many superbly constructed still lives are dotted around the apartment. Among the most notable are this shallow turquoise dish holding pears fabricated from old papers (below left) and a wonderful piece of antique coral with dramatic flamelike coloring that hangs in vibrant splendor against its dark background (below right). In another Paris home, a line of dried pomegranates are ranged casually in front of an aged firescreen (below center). The rich colors and textures are reminiscent of an Old Master painting.

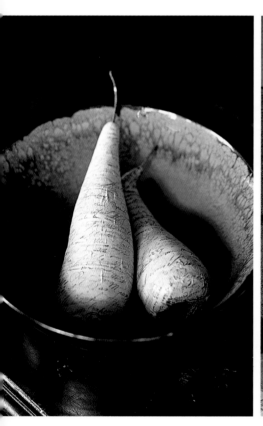

IN MANY THINGS NATURE REMAINS ABUNDANT. TREES OFFER UP A BOUNTY OF FALLEN LEAVES, NUTS, SEEDCASES, BERRIES, AND BRANCHES THAT IS AN ENDLESS SOURCE OF DECORATIVE DELIGHT.

NATURE'S BOUNTY Here a charming miniature still life (right), part of a larger display, unites a fistful of dried oak leaves with a wooden acorn in a witty visual pun. The leaves are a favorite motif, recurring throughout the illustrator's home in which they are to be found. These are particularly handsome specimens, carefully pressed and dried to preserve them perfectly. In the house of a constant globetrotter (below), a casual handful of natural finds—seedcases and leaves—contains just a hint of the exotic in the shape of a tiny beaded lizard—a most unexpected addition. The shallow glass bowl allows the forms to be appreciated from any viewpoint.

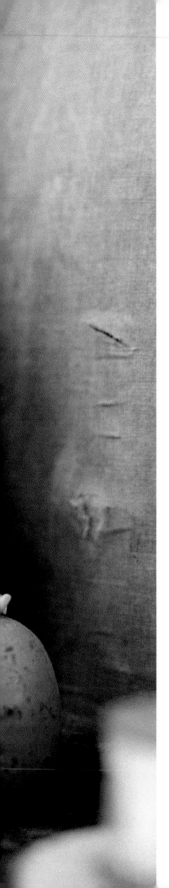

NATURAL FINDS A leaf in a state of decay is still an object of interest and beauty. Sitting alone in a very contemporary vessel, the texture and form of this large leaf can be enjoyed and appreciated (right). A mirror-backed window frame has been converted into an unusual coffee table, and one of its divisions is devoted to feathers and shells (below right).

The wonders of the natural world influence and inspire much man-made design. It's no surprise then that many of us covet the magical forms we encounter on a walk in the woods or an expedition to exotic shores. However, it's important to be aware that while nature is regenerative, it is not invincible. The arrogance and ignorance of past generations, who greedily plundered natural resources and treasures, mean that today we all have a duty to preserve endangered areas and items of the natural world, rather than adding to the crisis. Therefore, even the most tempting of vacation tokens, such as shells, pebbles, and coral, should not be removed from the beach. Be aware that similar purchased souvenirs may have arrived on the sales floor by erroneous or even illegal means, so they should be avoided. Vintage coral, like antique ivory, is exonerated owing to its age and provides one avenue to go down if these materials or forms are just too tempting to resist.

However, in many things, nature remains abundant, and bringing home certain *objets trouvés* is pleasurable and uncontroversial. Trees offer up a generous bounty of fallen leaves, nuts, seedcases, berries, and branches that are an endless source of decorative delight. Passing birds preen and discard their feathers for us to find and be enchanted by. Butterflies and bugs lie resplendent, willing to be captured once their short lives have ceased. And fruits and flowers enjoy our continued admiration as they dry to fascinating, papery imitations of their former selves.

Packaging is a multimillion-dollar business. In our mass-market consumerist society, a product must persuade us to purchase it rather than one of its rivals. To this end, packaging strives to seduce us into picking it up off the shelves. Often, we are attracted to the exterior regardless of the content—proof of the power of great design.

Nowadays, paper shopping bags are popular collectibles. Glossy and luxurious, with cord or ribbon handles, these disposable items are status symbols in their own right. Many people visit a prestigious store to buy the cheapest item and walk away with their purchase wrapped in the store's signature packaging and popped in a coveted bag. And often this packaging is so appealing that it deserves to be displayed at home. Shopping bags can swing from the closet door, or be arranged on the floor in formation and used to store bits and pieces. Attractive boxes look striking stacked in a building-block formation in glass-fronted cupboards and cabinets. Display attractive

packaging and memorabilia

OLDE-WORLDE CHARM This illustrator's home is a haven of whimsical delight. The shelves are crammed with inspirational finds with a characterful past (opposite page). Battered tins are interspersed with witty ephemera picked up along the way. The effect is less confusing than expected, owing to the simple color scheme. The owner's love of red and white made these first-aid boxes great finds (above right). They sit happily on top of an armoire and house a collection of hats. A collection of food lockers have found a home in the bathroom (right), where they offer both decorative effects and practical storage. A quiet corner is home to a stack of old magazines and an ever-changing display of much-loved family photographs (far right).

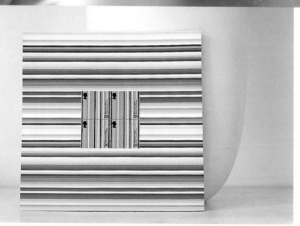

PLEASINGLY PATTERNED (PREVIOUS SPREAD) Long after their contents have been consumed or discarded, tins can continue to be utilized; and their shapes, colors, and patterns can continue to be enjoyed. In a London house (right), an old cabinet has been lined in geometric-patterned paper to create a crazy, clashing backdrop for an assortment of boldly patterned tins. A more subtle arrangement of boxes and tins are used as storage receptacles on open shelves (below left), while a harmonious family of bottles, boxes, and tins display a collection of labels with similar olde-worlde charm (above left). A tower of matchboxes offers endless opportunities for fiddling and rearranging (center).

food containers on kitchen shelves and arrange color-coordinated labels on boxes, bottles, and tins to form still lifes that enchant the eye.

The passage of time somehow imbues even the most mundane objects with a sentimental appeal. Old photographs, letters, postcards, invitations, magazines, tickets, and labels…the flotsam and jetsam of other people's lives represents a veritable treasure trove. A theater lover might want to collect and display tickets or programs of past productions. For others the same items may have a purely visual or typographical appeal. Old photographs are a marvelous piece of social history, offering a fascinating insight into changing fashions and conventions from the Victorian era on. In 1839, two exciting new inventions, daguerreotypes and calotypy, first became available. From those early techniques, the medium has developed and flourished, becoming increasingly sophisticated in recent years. Today, even those objects that move too fast or too far for the human eye can be captured on film.

Sadly, although Victorian frames have been popular for some years, the photographs that they originally contained were often discarded. However, the products of many commercial Victorian photographers and

PICTURE POSTCARDS We don't have to rely on friends to send us postcards—nowadays there is a wonderful choice of vintage and contemporary cards to choose from. Sets of cards that share a theme are worth looking for. Here (opposite page), a set of 1950s "a girl and her dog" cards have been varnished and put into use as a witty splashback behind a kitchen sink. In a bathroom (above and right), a group of old-fashioned seaside postcards and photos have been brought together to create an apt display. When a lively striped postage stamp was issued in England, a London stylist couldn't resist finding a similarly stripey piece of card to mount them on (opposite page, below).

A FEAST FOR THE EYES Packaging from around the world often appeals on a purely visual level, regardless of its contents. The tin may contain some obscure medicinal remedy or unknown spice, but the image on the container makes it immediately appealing. Here (this page and opposite page), a small shelf unit is filled with lively tins and packets from distant lands. Some have been purchased on trips abroad, while others were found in local grocers or foodstores that specialize in exotic produce. The tower of nylon pan scourers adds a further splash of color.

NOTEWORTHY An obsession with typography is easily satisfied now packaging design has become so seductive. Vast sums are spent on marketing beauty products, and the packaging can prove too pleasing to discard (below left). When it comes to fashion, bags bearing the names of stylish designers and stores are just as coveted as their contents (below center). In a New York loft, this neon graffiti by a renowned artist is a quote from James Joyce (below right). Magnetic letters are a shade more chic when the alphabet is in elegant script (right). A collection of old retail sign lettering is both graphic and whimsical (opposite page).

portrait studios can still be found in curio shops or procured from specialized dealers. Between 1868 and 1914, promenade, boudoir, panel, and coupon prints became available, as well as the picture postcard, which rapidly gained in popularity. "Real photograph" postcards were still produced in the 1950s.

Postcards are fascinating, not only for their images, but for their written messages and decorative stamps. There are many possibilities for display. You could collect images of your home town or local area and display them in your hall, providing a fascinating overview of the gradually changing face of a street or neighborhood over the years. Perhaps you love animals and could start a collection of cards of cats or dogs, or even frogs or pigs! Similarly, you could devise a visual theme that suggests placement in a particular room. Beach and water subjects on display in a bathroom, for example, are pleasingly appropriate.

THE PASSAGE OF TIME IMBUES EVEN THE MOST MUNDANE OBJECTS WITH A SENTIMENTAL APPEAL.

NEVER JUDGE A BOOK BY ITS COVER An ultra-minimal and pared-down chimney breast and fireplace is the resting place of a set of 1950s books (left). The charm of these bookclub issues resides in their covers, which share a unifying design of zodiacal symbols and signs, each in a slightly different color. Although dog-eared and faded now, the collection is greatly appealing and brings a splash of unexpected color and interest to a simply furnished room.

books

In today's world of information overload, the television and computer offer an immediate and animated alternative to the pleasures of a book. But books offer a dual reward: the cerebral and the material—something of beauty both inside and out.

From the illuminated manuscripts of medieval monks to the high-tech mechanical replication processes of the modern day, books have chronicled the history of the civilized world, reporting the mood and manners of every era. By the time Queen Victoria came to the throne, the printed word had become more accessible, owing to the development of the automated printing press in 1830. Famous artists turned their talents to illustrating the popular novels of the day, and many volumes from this era have stunning engravings, sometimes hand-tinted.

It was not until 1930, when the American Ira Rubel's offset lithography printing was combined with a system for introducing colored inks, that mass-production color printing became possible. Children's books and illustrated reference works benefited from this technological breakthrough. Today, computer-generated pages are laser printed with unprecedented definition. At the same time there is increased interest in limited print runs and handcrafted volumes.

BOOKS GALORE   In this unique Paris home (above), the double height of the room has been used to house a two-tiered wall of bookshelves. Movable steps, in the library tradition, provide the photographer owner of the apartment with access to the higher levels, which are packed with tomes on design. For added visual stimulation, unusual artefacts are interspersed with books on the lower shelves. The confined space in a New York residence has resulted in the additional use of an open staircase as a place for a growing collection of books (top right), while another Manhattan home finds the family cat enjoying the sun on top of a pile of oversize art books on the deep windowsills of this old warehouse (above right).

ANY WHICH WAY Books are stackable, and any surface can offer a home to a display of well-loved novels or ancient tomes. In a Paris apartment, a set of ancient African stools are piled high with books (opposite page, left). In another, more eclectic Paris home, books are heaped on seating and spill into haphazard groups on any available floor space (above left), offering display space for numerous eccentric treasures. Old books have a beauty that is not diminished by their battered state, making them a pleasing addition to any room (above right).

Books are wonderfully collectible. Not many people can afford to invest in rare first editions or antique tomes, although the handsomeness of their hand-stitched and vellum-bound covers is undisputable. A more affordable area is that of vintage paperbacks, which are now becoming big business, thanks to their bold and dramatic cover designs and typography. Classic children's titles, in the shape of both picture and storybooks, are also increasingly popular.

If your favorite book illustrations are too beautiful to remain hidden, display the book open on a small easel, desktop lectern, shelf, or tabletop so the contents can be admired by all who pass by. If it's the books and their bindings you value rather than the illustrations, make them a focal point of your interior. Stack them on a specially built grid of shelves or a bold bookcase. Display particular favorites on sideboards, coffee tables, chairs—even the floor. Pile books high on every conceivable surface—stools or steps, alcoves, or armchairs.

If your library sits upon shelves, it's sensible to organize the contents in some way. There are as many options as there are titles. Bibliophiles hotly debate whether to categorize books by subject matter or to arrange them alphabetically by title or by author. A less orthodox but more successful visual solution is to group books within publishing houses as this results in strong blocks of color from the identical spines.

how to
display

ROVING REPTILES To create a display that never fails to amuse is a real achievement. In a London home, a passion for reptiles is evident as they reappear throughout the house in the most surprising and entertaining fashion (above and opposite page).

how to display

There are no hard and fast rules about what you do in your own space with your own possessions, there are only guidelines—and they can often be ignored, with very successful results! Some people are totally uninhibited about what they put on display and how they do it. Others are woefully intimidated about how, where, and what to display. In this book I hope to enlighten and assist them. So, cupboards and cardboard boxes, drawers and desks, attics and armoires everywhere can be opened with anticipation, and the contents brought out to see the light of day.

Art galleries, museums, stores, and visits to different countries and cultures, as well as other people's homes, can inspire and inform your display decisions. Family

photographs may work well in a formation you remember from a art gallery you once visited. A house pictured in a glossy magazine might spark your imagination when it comes to positioning your hat collection. But remember that successful displays are always a work in progress—their transient nature is part of their appeal.

Where should you start? I'd suggest emptying shelves, display cabinets, mantelpieces, windowsills, and table tops, and collecting all your treasures together. Now put aside your very special pieces, the ones that make your heart sing with pleasure or pride. Place all items of a similar color in another group. There will probably be a collection that falls neatly

SPOTTED The lizard theme displays plenty of humorous touches. Lizards scuttle up the hall walls (above right) and hide behind the bathroom mirror (opposite page, left). They look spookily lifelike perched on cacti (center) or nestling among rocks (above left).

into a thematic subdivision. There will also be lots of things that no longer seem relevant to your life or your taste. Don't hesitate to discard them. Now take a look at what you have left in front of you.

You need to showcase your special treasures successfully. A large item, like a gilt mirror or a dressmaker's dummy, could be displayed in your living room, where you can enjoy it every time you sink into the sofa. Larger pieces have more impact alone, whereas smaller items are lent more consequence when displayed *en masse*. If your most treasured possession is a collection of glass bottles, they'll have a much stronger presence grouped together than dotted around several rooms.

Small-scale treasures of a varying nature should be arranged on a coffee table or kitchen windowsill or by the phone—anywhere they can be admired at close quarters, and regularly rearranged as part of an enjoyable ritual. Take a handful of items, decide on their new home, and settle down to an hour of happy contemplation. Pick up and put down, rearrange and re-jig, fiddle and tinker to your heart's content.

You'll end up with a pile of miscellaneous bits and pieces that don't seem to fit together. Perfect! Eclectic combinations never fail to draw the eye. Be brave—put that kitsch plastic Elvis clock next to that delicate bone china teapot Grandma gave you—and you'll create a talking point, if nothing else!

Symmetry vs. asymmetry

There are many options when it comes to positioning pieces for display. A group of identical bowls will suit a symmetrical placing at regular intervals, with like balancing like. With a group of objects that are all the same color, size, and shape, there's little to be gained from an asymmetric configuration—a single bowl would not justify placement apart from its shelfmates— it won't balance the others and will just look sorry for itself. However, symmetry is not just about identical items. The eye will also accept as symmetrical a group that is balanced. It will balance two large objects even if they are not mirror images of each other, and two different colors if they are of a similar tone.

WELL BALANCED Though they're not symmetrical, there is a happy balance to these shelves that pleases the eye (right). The unusual wall-mounted speakers create an impression of symmetry within their vertical confines, but in fact each shelf is quite different in its content and arrangement, although the overall effect is undeniably harmonious. A set of carved-wood Indonesian heads (above) mounted on slender posts is set beside very different counterparts—a trio of tall wooden ninepins. Despite the differences in color and proportion, the group forms a united whole, demonstrating that asymmetric arrangements can be just as balanced as symmetric ones.

CENTRAL FOCUS In the home of a New York sculptor, every nook and cranny reveals her creative spirit. A side table, picture, and coat rack (right) are lined up between two large windows, in a deliberately symmetrical fashion. The curlicued table legs are echoed in the swirls of the painting, and the dangling collection of crucifixes just brushes the very top of the artwork. On the table sits a tableau of personal treasures. Another area of the same loft finds an unusual presentation of an old bilge pump cover (below right), its subtle coloration of similar tone to the distressed paintwork covering a chest of drawers that holds a curvaceous vintage lamp.

Stacking a pile of bowls at one end of a mantelpiece, and leaving the rest of the surface bare would be a contemporary asymmetric approach. If you like, the stacked bowls could be balanced by one or two larger or more brightly colored items set at the other end of the mantelpiece. This approach works on exactly the same principle as weighing scales, where one large weight is equal to or balances several smaller ones. It's common sense, really.

A random grouping of objects united only by color or texture has no obvious symmetry within its arrangement. Position such collections asymmetrically on a shelf or tabletop. Arrangements that are allowed to evolve organically are also invariably asymmetric, owing to the gradual development of the display and the varying objects it contains. You rarely find two identical pieces of rock or buy vases in duplicate, while a retro piece is often a one-off.

A single picture or mirror propped on a mantelpiece can look just as impressive placed in the center as on one side. The dynamics are different, but both arrangements present an equally pleasing solution. The preference lies purely in the eye of the beholder. There are no rights and wrongs—if it gratifies you, an object can be displayed upside down and back to front, too!

MIX AND MATCH Play with pattern, form, and color for dynamic display effects. A striped glass bottle almost vanishes when placed on similarly patterned pink and white linen (above left), while handtowels in vibrant shades complement the colorful chair they sit on (above center). Spots and diamonds are linked by their bold primary colors (above right). Mellow clouded glass reflects rusting ironwork on bare boards for an atmospheric effect (below left). The texture of a multitude of corks is distorted by the faceted finish of the glass vases that hold them (below center). The fragility of an antique tutu is highlighted by cracked paintwork on an old door (below right). All these examples demonstrate the wealth of options open to us when it comes to how and where we display our personal possessions, however small and insignificant they may appear.

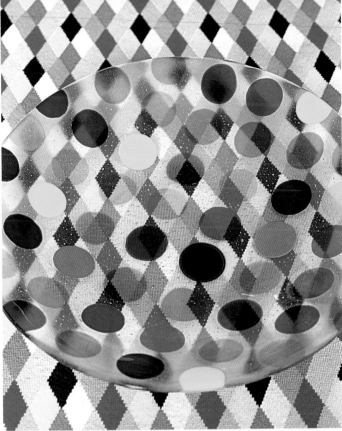

Color, texture, and contrast

When it comes to display, the power of color should never be underestimated. Adding one strong, zingy color to a harmonious neutral grouping will immediately draw the eye away from the rest. In effect, it creates an asymmetric display, even when the objects on show are otherwise identical.

A device called the color wheel shows that color combinations can be harmonious or complementary. Colors that sit next to each other on the wheel—purple and blue, or cream and yellow, for example—make pleasingly harmonious combinations. Colors that are positioned opposite each other on the wheel—blue and yellow or red and green—clash and contrast, bringing drama and vitality to arrangements.

The use of chiaroscuro (which means "clear-obscure" or "light-shade" in Italian) in paintings demonstrates the effectiveness of contrast. A dark object will stand out dramatically when placed against a bright or white background. Conversely, a dark or muted background will throw pale or glowing colors into bold relief.

Texture can provide a link or a contrast in the same way as color. A floaty chemise hung against peeling paintwork is a perfect mismatch, persuading the eye to appreciate the different attributes of each item. Color and texture are often in league to bring us mouth-watering effects. The richness of intensely colored dyes and paint techniques combined with intricate patterns or sumptuous embroidery makes for a visual extravaganza. Some countries, such as India or China, are particularly prolific in their expressive use of pattern and color, and can suggest new or unexpected ways of combining color and texture.

LITTLE AND LARGE The most inconsequential, even the most uninspiring areas of your home possess remarkable display possibilities. In a New York warehouse, the utility pipes and fuse box may seem a strange focus for a delicate ballet performance, but the little ledges provide an unexpected stage for just such a miniature presentation (above). The impression is that of a modern cityscape (far left), but in fact these are small blocks of wood placed randomly on a narrow table. In a similar display, tiny wooden bricks are placed alongside an imposing wooden vase, juxtaposing large and small (left). In a Paris living area, a long framework of metal girders is home to a display of old postcards that are treasured for their messages (opposite page, above). A tiny key looks even more miniscule nailed to a large expanse of door (opposite page, below).

Playing with scale

Diversity of scale makes for stimulating displays. A variety in scale within a composition helps the eye to move around a group instead of skimming over a more uniform arrangement. Placing a large object next to a small one accentuates and emphasizes each one's size. Put a tiny pair of children's shoes among a row of adult-sized ones and they stand out instantly, to a chorus of adoring exclamations. Range a row of miniature teapots in front of a full-sized line-up. Break up a shelf of oversized books with smaller ones that have been stacked on their side to interrupt the uniformity. Surround a large picture with smaller satellite images arranged in a spectacular starburst configuration. You'll find that these intriguing juxtapositions will draw and delight the eye.

Positioning can bring scale into play. A tiny item nailed to the back of a door is immediately set in its own enormous border. A huge painting hung on a wall that's only a little larger helps the eye appreciate the proportions of both room and painting.

Ultimately, when it comes to creating displays, you are limited only by your own imagination. There is no display too eccentric and no combination too eclectic if the components are a source of pleasure. Place the unexpected where the expected once sat and the expected in an unexpected position. Experiment with fun new ideas. Amuse yourself by changing the function and location of objects—the saucepan stand from the kitchen makes a perfect book shelf in the living room. A little lateral thinking goes a long way when you are striving for the perfect display, but always keep your sense of humor. If you find rearranging your shelves preferable to a night out, you may be taking things just a shade too seriously!

MAKING ARRANGEMENTS In a room dedicated to the color pink, a cluster of objects sits on a coffee table (opposite page, right). The sugar-pink shell is the dominant piece, owing to its remarkable size. A shell-shaped glass dish continues the theme. A slender, opaque glass bottle adds height, while other glass pieces bring varying tints of pink to the arrangement. A small still life is united by color (opposite page, left). The crackle-glazed ceramic egg, soapstone dish, bonbon, and fabric rose are all delicate shades of pink. A collection of ceramic dachshunds is guaranteed to raise a smile (left), whereas a carefully considered arrangement of varying textures and shapes simply pleases the eye (below left). An collection of African stools and statuettes occupies a tabletop (below right).

still lifes

The term "still life" immediately conjures up an image of a gloomy Old Master painting of fruit and flowers on a pewter platter. Artworks featuring inanimate objects within a domestic setting is, in fact, the dictionary definition. But in the context of successful display, a still life is a feast for the eye, a carefully considered arrangement of objects within a given space that sit happily together. It's all to do with achieving harmony of form, color, and texture.

Restricting yourself to a limited color range is one of the easiest ways to start a still life. Select a few items and play around with them until the arrangement pleases your eye. When you are happy with the composition, add a dash of the unexpected to liven it up. Incorporating several touches of the same color will relate each piece to its neighbor and lead the eye around the group. Choosing a plain background for an arrangement of unusual shapes will give them more impact. Even the most beautiful of objects can be enhanced by the right backdrop or surroundings. By introducing a new element to a mix—something unexpected, even downright bizarre—the dynamics of a still life can be altered dramatically. Don't take it too seriously—there is no right or wrong when it comes to these decorative displays, but learning to balance a small group of vases or other favored objects is a fun and satisfying accomplishment.

Once these principles are in your mind, you will find yourself pausing while closing the curtains to rearrange the contents of the windowsill or fiddling with the lineup on your mantelpiece while chatting on the phone. When placed together in a sympathetic way, a jumble of disparate objects becomes a display that is more interesting than the sum of its parts. This is the aim of a still life—to take pieces from the everyday world and make something a lot less ordinary.

IT'S SHOWTIME! Objects of fragile beauty, these creamy ceramic flowerheads are displayed on the open pages of an ancient, hand-scribed book (opposite page). Equally intriguingly, the inside of an old book has been cut out to provide a home for a love heart, creating a suggestion of a secret attachment (below left). These elegant, elongated Asian hands are accompanied by a vase of leaves with similar fingerlike fronds (below center). In a New York office, an impressively neat desk displays office and art equipment stashed in a group of decorative green ceramics, all contained within the confines of a black lacquered tray (below right).

WHEN PLACED TOGETHER IN A SYMPATHETIC WAY, A JUMBLE OF DISPARATE OBJECTS BECOMES
A DECORATIVE DISPLAY THAT IS MORE INTERESTING THAN THE SUM OF ITS PARTS.

freestanding supports

ALTERED IMAGES Liberated from the confines of the kitchen, this pan stand provides shelving for a collection of various volumes (right). Occupying little floor space, it holds favorite books on perpetual display and keeps them close at hand where they can be enjoyed on a regular basis. In a Paris work space, a lofty wooden ladder, possessing a certain aesthetic appeal in itself, holds a number of free-falling measuring tapes, which spiral down around the rungs (opposite page). In a London home, a music stand has been commandeered to provide a home for several old photograph albums (above). A large sturdy stand like this one is a great find, not to mention extremely versatile. The display possibilities are endless, and the stand would make an ideal home for a number of different items—pictures, open books, even sheet music. The smaller stand could also sit happily on a desk or side table.

SOME THINGS DESIGNED
ESPECIALLY FOR ONE
PURPOSE MAY SURPRISE YOU
WITH THEIR ADAPTABILITY.
ALL THAT'S NEEDED IS A
LITTLE LATERAL THINKING.

Some things designed specifically for one purpose may surprise you with their adaptability. An umbrella stand could accommodate a collection of driftwood. The hall hatstand could migrate to the bedroom and show off a collection of vintage dresses. A tiered pan stand might house a treasured tea set. An old ladder simply begs to have textiles or even more obscure items draped over its rungs. Or a humble stepladder could be pressed into service as a shelving system. All that's needed is a little lateral thinking.

In exactly the same way that a bookshelf is the best place to hold books, a dressmaker's dummy must surely be the most suitable way to display clothes. Vintage wire stands with tiny waists and flared hips are appealing in their own right. Mannequins, especially the truncated versions used by milliners, are an equally appropriate means of displaying fashion in the home. And wooden hat blocks are perfect supports for collections of headgear, from tiaras to top hats.

Music stands are perfect receptacles for photographs, artworks, or books—any object that can be propped on the narrow ledge they offer. A multibranched floor stand can take you to display heaven. Easels are an ideal way to show off paintings. Old easels that once held school blackboards can be found in secondhand stores, while more refined versions from auction houses or art galleries are a more expensive investment. Look out for scaled-down versions that can perch on a tabletop and carry a small painting or open book.

REST EASY Once home to a child's blackboard, this small easel now displays a romantic floral painting (left). The beauty of displaying pictures on an easel is that they can be changed as the mood takes you. Wooden hat blocks are the ideal place for displaying a collection of favorite hats (above left).

FASHIONABLE FORMS A spectacular creation that demands to be appreciated in all its three-dimensional glory can only be shown off to perfection on a tailor's dummy or mannequin, where its form and presence can be revealed. Here, an exuberant concoction of net adorned with colorful silk flowers twists around the body and draws the eye in all its vivid splendor (left). A vintage mannequin, with an elegant swanlike neck that has been elongated to exaggerated proportions, has come straight from the hat-shop window to display a cherished chapeau (below).

furniture and display units

SITTING COMFORTABLY Odd chairs, flea-market or yard-sale finds chosen for their good looks rather than their comfort rating, can become part of a sensational display. A row of old theater seats have been revamped in elaborate satin brocade and sit thronelike, a row of plump, plush, buttoned footstools in luscious shades of velvet kneeling at their feet (opposite page). Eye-catching in their own right, they also provide a showcase for a collection of colorful handbags. In a Paris apartment, two large ceramic dishes perch like cushions on a surplus chair (above), while a love of designer chairs has resulted in this lineup of child-sized versions in a New York loft (above right). An original Eames cabinet provides a fitting backdrop.

Some pieces of furniture can become a passion. A long hall is the ideal location for a row of decorative chairs that you adore, but which are not comfortable enough for daily use. A love of designer chairs can be more easily accommodated if you limit yourself to collecting miniature versions. Alternatively, you could mount full-sized chairs on the wall Shaker–style, using the traditional peg rail.

Certain chairs are so decorative that they make wonderful display items in themselves, but chairs can also double as display units. A row of unused dining chairs could be used to show off a collection of unusual handbags or decorative paper shopping bags.

In the Victorian era, occasional and side tables heaved with a fascinating array of decorative objects. Apart from the coffee table, the contemporary home is

PERFECT PLACEMENT In the corner of a Paris home and work space, a large primitive wooden bowl sits on an old metal office stool that acts as the perfect pedestal (above left). A home full of wit and charm finds an upholstered Victorian desk chair with strangely elongated legs is just the place to position an equally beguiling (and unusual) metal handbag. Other curios surround the scene, adding to its fascination (above right). This long, low-line sideboard, sitting alongside a bare brick wall in a New York loft, bears a small podium, which gives a select grouping of mid-century American ceramics a sense of added importance (right).

GETTING ON TOP OF THINGS In a Manhattan apartment that reveals a passion for the interior decor of the 1970s, a collection of Pyrex dishes dating from that era has been gradually amassed during visits to bric-à-brac and flea markets (below). The collection has a Scandinavian-style transfer print in orange and turquoise and occasionally goes out on show. A handmade rice basket from the Philippines doubles as an occasional table to hold an understated trio of Swedish ceramics from the 1950s and 1980s (left). The rich, dark coloring of all the pieces makes this a very subtle display of contrasting textures.

more likely to adopt a long, low bench, a windowsill, or a simple stool to hold special pieces.

Traditional display furniture such as hutches should not be dismissed as too countrified for the contemporary urban home. Rustic, simply painted French or Scandinavian versions can work well in a modern interior if they are kept from becoming too cluttered or conventional. A selection of plain white china would look austerely impressive, as would a collection of old pewter platters. Even paperbacks or children's books can sit on the narrow shelves.

Shelf units are the ideal way to display your treasures to their best advantage. Look for freestanding, custom-made, or purchased shelving that can be extended as your collection of prized possessions expands. The popularity of the grid of open box shelves is understandable, since it allows different themes to be displayed in different compartments. Some cubicles can be stacked high with books or crammed with ceramics, while others can contain a single showpiece, the overall effect being an abstract pattern, like movable wallpaper.

BUILT FOR THE JOB Predominantly glass, this cabinet (above) is a great find for displaying assorted objects that appeal to and inspire its photographer owner. A 1970s display unit takes pride of place in this New York apartment (opposite page, left). It holds a selection of pottery of a similar vintage as well as the TV and music system it was designed to house. This wall of gridded shelves (opposite page, right) has an informal unity, with books above and below an impressive collection of Russel Wright tableware.

STORE UNIT FITTINGS ARE DESIGNED EXPRESSLY TO DISPLAY THEIR CONTENTS. AFTER MANY YEARS IN A RETAIL ENVIROMENT, THEY CAN MAKE THE TRANSITION TO A DOMESTIC INTERIOR VERY SUCCESSFULLY.

In the 1960s and 1970s, the wall unit became an essential component of any groovy pad. It played a multifunctional role, acting in both a storage and display capacity and incorporating both open shelves and closed glass-fronted cabinets. As with many modern classics, the wall unit is currently enjoying a renaissance. It offers the perfect opportunity for display and so is well worth considering—go for either an original design or a modern version.

Store unit fittings are designed expressly to display their contents. After many years in a retail enviroment, they can make the transition to a domestic interior very successfully. Customize them by painting the insides to complement or contrast with the contents.

When displaying your precious pieces in a smaller container, transparency is the key element. Clear vases, pitchers, and jars made from plastic, plexiglass, and glass can all be filled with eye-catching treasures. The science laboratory is a fertile hunting ground for small-scale display possibilities—glass specimen jars and test tubes come in interesting shapes and sizes. The Victorian bell jar was specifically designed to cover and protect while allowing a view of its contents. These glass jars are now rare and consequently expensive, but nineteenth-century glass cloches from the garden are a good substitute. Even better, modern reproductions in both glass and plastic exist as very affordable alternatives to the often elusive Victorian originals.

ceilings and suspension

HANGING ON IN THERE The workshop table in the home of a New York sculptor has assorted nuts, bolts, cogs, and metal washers suspended from one end on elongated wire s-hooks, all awaiting use in her creations but meanwhile forming an intriguing display in their own right (left). The technique could be adapted successfully to hang many different objects. A handful of kitchen spoons are slotted onto a nail in this Paris kitchen. Their display is both practical—keeping them close at hand while cooking—and modern (opposite page, above right). The New York home of a musical family has a primitive musical instrument hanging from one of the heavy wood and metal beams of the loft's original framework (opposite page, below left). Disposable styrofoam cups have been imaginatively recycled into spherical lampshades that echo the circular stucco designs that adorn the apartment ceiling. This novel light covering shows what can be achieved with clever ideas and little cash (opposite page, below right).

When you look around a room to assess its display potential, it generally tends to be eye level and below that is the main focus of one's attention. However, if you also consider the ceiling, an whole new world of display possibilities are suddenly opened up.

Suspending items is a particularly suitable method of display for anything that is best appreciated as a three-dimensional object. Even better, suspension offers an exciting opportunity to create an idiosyncratic statement within a room. Pieces of salvaged machinery, for example, can create an amazing abstract sculpture that keeps people guessing as to their previous identity.

Ceiling mobiles deserve to be reconsidered, as many can be fabulously funky. Try your hand at creating a customized version. If you are something of a calligrapher, inscribe poetry quotes on blank postcards, have them laminated, then punch holes in them and

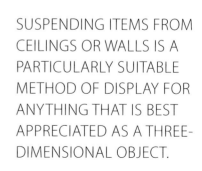

SUSPENDING ITEMS FROM CEILINGS OR WALLS IS A PARTICULARLY SUITABLE METHOD OF DISPLAY FOR ANYTHING THAT IS BEST APPRECIATED AS A THREE-DIMENSIONAL OBJECT.

EYE-CATCHING EFFECTS In a vibrant yellow room, a mirrored doorback is home to a robe of deep violet (right). There is more bold use of color on the ceiling of this New York loft, which has been given a coat of candy-pink paint and bedecked with an assortment of pretty, twinkling chandeliers (opposite page). No attempt has been made to hide the pipes or remove the modern strip lighting, and the incongruous combination is very eccentric. The tiniest displays are often the most enchanting. Here, a single cut-glass drop hangs from a ribbon, catching the light as it moves in the breeze (above).

suspend them from invisible thread. Alternatively, print the quotes off from a computer in a decorative font. This also works well for favorite photographs.

Ornamental light fixtures, such as candelabras, can multiply extravagantly above your head, whether or not they are actually wired up and working. More functional lighting doesn't have to be dull. Hanging several lights of varying length together in a cluster creates a very modern effect. Try suspending five small lights over a dining table, for example. Antique birdcages in wire or wicker look whimsical hanging from the ceiling. Feathered ornamental birds could reside in them rather than the real thing.

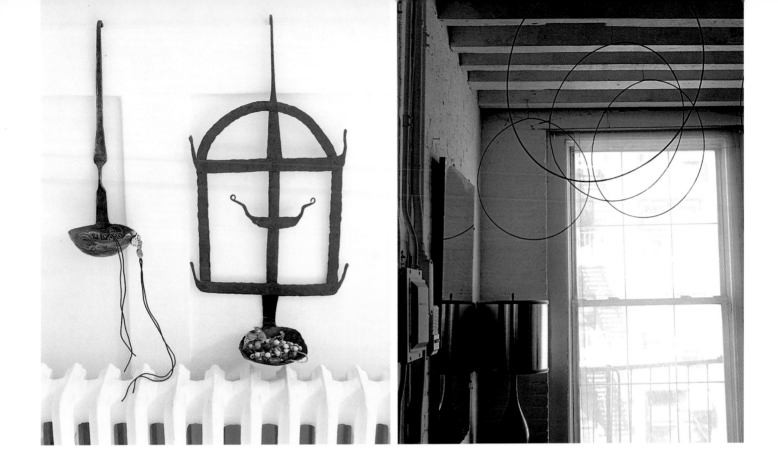

You don't have to hang your treasures from the ceiling. Any lip or ledge has scope for exploitation. The backs of chairs or the edge of tables, bannisters or headboards, door knobs or drawer handles—all these spots can double as display space when kitted out with a selection of ties or s-hooks.

Functional items can also be adapted for display purposes. An old-fashioned laundry drying rack could hold decorative items. Simple kitchen items such as mugs or pans are pleasingly decorative hanging from a Shaker peg rail or a minimalist set of steel hooks. A length of string and a few clothespins will allow you to create temporary displays in any room. Children can brighten up the kitchen or the hall with an exhibition of their latest artwork, while you can decorate your bedroom with favorite *billets-doux*.

GETTING THE HANG OF IT In an old warehouse in Manhattan, now a living space, the ceiling carries a group of large and slender metal hoops. It is a most unexpected element of informality in an otherwise traditionally furnished corner, but the display creates a feeling of movement and magically invigorates the atmosphere of the whole space (opposite page and above right). In a London home, Indian metalware collected on exotic travels has been suspended from the top of painted paneling (above). Shiny scissors in several different sizes hang from a hook in the kitchen of a Paris architect who enjoys their form (right). Repetition of a simple motif can be a very effective device when it comes to creating successful displays.

THE CENTER OF ATTENTION

Very much the focal point of a New York living space, this traditional-style fireplace has been devoted to a collection of contemporary ceramics (right). The subdued wall color is the same as the base color of the vessels, while a splash of vivid turquoise is introduced in the shape of less sophisticated pieces of rustic pottery. A specially commissioned firescreen adds to the visual interest. Although a similar color scheme is used in a London apartment (opposite page), the feel, in contrast, is starkly minimal. Carefully placed at one end of the mantelpiece is a set of raku pots in the same dull-brown tone. The starkness is relieved by a frivolous pair of silver slippers.

mantelpieces

Once upon a time, the mantelpiece was the central focus of a room, owing to the fact that the fireplace was the primary source of heat. Traditionally, the mantelpiece had a visual theme that was repeated in thousands of households throughout the land. Either side of a central clock, in a perfectly symmetrical line-up, was a candlestick and vase combination with a china figurine at each end, and a mirror or picture hanging above. This formula still holds true in many homes, but, when it is liberated from such conventions, the possibilities for mantelpiece display are endless.

With the advent of central heating, the fireplace was no longer the focus of a room. Many fireplaces were filled in and mantelpieces removed, made redundant by the radiator. However, many contemporary homes have reinstated the deposed fire surround, simply

ON THE LINE The mantelpiece is all too often a tempting home for all and sundry, but less clutter can result in more appealing effects. Here, the most minimal of arrangements is perched to one side of the mantelshelf, while favorite bits and pieces are pinned along a length of string, in a casual yet considered display (this page). This solution to displaying ephemera is particularly appropriate for an understated modern mantelpiece such as this one.

MODERN VERSUS TRADITIONAL Conventional mantelpieces do not necessarily warrant conventional displays. A nineteenth-century marble mantelpiece is home to a row of wire busts (right), while berry-hued glass sits on a similarly grand example (below right). Minimal does not equal modern. Here an empty gilt frame sits alone on a mantelpiece (above).

because it offers such a useful central focus for a room. If you don't have a fireplace and mantelpiece, you can create a similar effect by putting a deep shelf on the wall at mantelpiece height. To prevent the shelf from looking isolated, position it between alcoves or cupboards, where a fireplace might once have stood.

A mantelpiece offers ample opportunity for experimentation. If you prefer the casual approach, allow various objects—postcards, invitations, photos—to accrue, documenting daily events and changing as elements are added and removed. A random grouping of disparate pieces often results in a successful display that all the arranging in the world cannot achieve.

The mantelpiece also offers a location to indulge in a more formal display that is linked by color, shape, or texture. Elegant arrangements can be formed and reformed. A bare mantelpiece is not an option, even in the most minimalist interior. Instead, a select group of objects or even a single piece, placed off center, will excite the eye with its stunning simplicity.

A BARE MANTELPIECE IS NOT AN OPTION. INSTEAD, A GROUP OF OBJECTS OR EVEN A SINGLE PIECE, PLACED OFF CENTER, WILL EXCITE THE EYE WITH ITS STUNNING SIMPLICITY.

windows

While your home may or may not have a mantelpiece, there is no likelihood of it lacking that most fundamental of architectural features—the window, complete with numerous sills and ledges that offer every chance to indulge in some form of display.

A fanciful array of fashion accessories can sit happily on a window sill that doesn't receive the sun's direct rays. Hats, shoes, and bags are all decorative by nature and deserve to be shown off rather than stashed away in closets. Window catches can double as hooks to hold pretty belts and pieces of costume jewelry, while ledges can offer a home to a vintage frock swinging on a padded satin hanger. Sheer chiffon or lace dresses could even make an imaginative alternative to more conventional curtains.

For a window that receives the full force of the morning or afternoon sun, consider a collection of colored glass. When the light floods through the glass, it will disperse the jeweled colors on to walls and floors, casting an ethereal glow over the room.

There's a wealth of display opportunities at every window, no matter how small or large. You simply need to recognize and exploit their potential. Narrow crossbars or frames can cope with a line-up of tiny treasures, while deep sills can show off larger and bulkier pieces. Best of all, an arrangement in a window is one that can be enjoyed by passers-by just as much as by the inhabitants of the interior. Indeed, your awareness of this additional audience may inspire you to use your windows in an even more creative way.

EDGES AND LEDGES Every window ledge has the potential for some form of display. This collection of tiny doll's baskets is ideally placed on an old sash window frame (opposite page). Like most miniature items, the baskets have an undeniable appeal. Tucked into the corner of a windowpane are two exquisite little images, one hand-painted on glass, the relics of a Victorian magic lantern show (above). The panels look particularly striking with the sun shining through the glass and illuminating the delicate details and gentle colors. The panels can also be admired from the street outside.

WINDOW DISPLAYS Such an impressive collection of both vintage and contemporary Liberty-print shirts just couldn't be relegated to a chest of drawers (opposite page). They have great appeal for the London stylist who intrepidly tracked them down in thriftstores around Britain as well as on seasonal spending sprees at the famous store. They are on permanent display in the living room, hanging from window crossbars to act as a curtain, providing privacy as well as decoration. They can be enjoyed from outside, too. Proof that pictures don't have to hang on walls—in another London home (left), a picture propped on the windowsill shows a delicate feminine face peering over the back of a curvaceous chaise longue.

WINDOW CATCHES CAN DOUBLE AS HOOKS TO HOLD PRETTY BELTS AND PIECES OF COSTUME JEWELRY, WHILE LEDGES CAN OFFER A HOME TO A VINTAGE FROCK SWINGING ON A PADDED SATIN HANGER.

floors

Using an expanse of floor as a display space creates a deliberately casual effect and lends the display a transient and spontaneous feel.

For those who prefer an informal, relaxed attitude to decorating, the floor can provide a very satisfactory exhibition area. The edges of rooms, where the floor meets the walls, offer a flexible display space for all sorts of propped pieces, be it favorite framed photographs, artworks, or just a row of decorative frames. A few books or magazines casually stacked alongside the baseboard can slowly evolve into a border of skyscraper proportions. Shoes look great arranged in neat lines along the edges of the walls, like soldiers on parade. Oversize baskets and bowls look particularly effective arranged in a cluster, and they can double as storage. Large sturdy paper shopping bags with rope handles and attractive typography look decorative *en masse*—arrange them in a neat row and

STANDING ROOM ONLY On the wall, this series of paintings might compete with the custom-made cabinets, but on the floor they provide the perfect linear complement to a neat storage solution. The floor is the safest place for this vast wooden tray (opposite page, left). A few carefully chosen pieces add to its impact and make for a successful still life on a grand scale. These frames are deliberately empty to encourage the spectator to admire their elaborate moldings and decorative effects (opposite page, right). Arranging them on the floor creates a casual feel that contrasts with their faded grandeur.

they can double as storage space for glossy magazines or containers for an assortment of miscellaneous bits and pieces.

The only restrictions when utilizing floor space for display purposes are the practicalities involved. Obviously, an arrangement of fragile pieces positioned in a busy pathway is not going to be a sustainable display, but when the same group is moved to a quieter corner of the room, it can provide an unexpected and imaginative still life.

Think in terms of exhibition spaces and allow free-standing pieces the opportunity to be enjoyed in the round. Indoor sculptures are very much the trend for Modernist homes. Create your own large-scale talking point with rough-hewn rocks or salvaged metal pieces.

Old-fashioned display containers once used in stores were often produced in exaggerated size, either to create an eye-catching show or for storage purposes. Oversize food cans with interesting labeling or enormous apothecaries' bottles make attractive arrangements. Luxurious oversize floor cushions are another growing trend in the contemporary home. Use fabric remnants to cover large cushions and pouffes, and lounge at floor level in true Moorish fashion.

FLOOR SHOW Large and bulky containers are far better safely placed on the floor than precariously perched on a shelf that may not be able to cope with their weight. In this bathroom, light streams through the window onto a collection of large glass apothecary bottles holding exotic bath oils in vibrant colors (right). A designer's hall is alive with an exciting mix of patterns contributed by tiles, a stair runner, and wallpaper. Her distinctive, richly decorated handbags sit happily within this melange of color and pattern (opposite page).

FOR THOSE WHO PREFER AN INFORMAL, RELAXED
ATTITUDE TO DECORATING, THE FLOOR CAN PROVIDE
A VERY SATISFACTORY EXHIBITION AREA.

resources

ANTIQUES & VINTAGE-STYLE PIECES

ABC Carpet & Home
881-888 Broadway
New York, NY 10003
212-674-1144
www.abccarpet.com
Home furnishings, fabrics, carpets, and design accessories.

American Pottery Exchange
www.the-apx.com
Popular ceramics; includes Lu Ray, Russel Wright, Eva Ziesel, McCoy, Bauer, and many more.

Christie's
20 Rockefeller Plaza
New York, NY 10020
212-636-2000
www.christies.com
Public auctions.

EBay (Internet auctions)
www.ebay.com
Individual sellers, quality and prices vary, with every category of merchandise represented.

English Country Antiques
Snake Hollow Road
Bridgehampton, NY 11932
516-537-0606
Period country furniture in pine, plus decorative blue-and-white china.

Fishs Eddy
889 Broadway
New York, NY 10011
212-420-2090
Overstock supplies of Fifties-style china mugs, plates, bowls, etc.

Kitchen Sink Antiques
North Carolina 27613
www.kitchensinkantiques.com
Specializes in all periods of glassware, dinnerware, kitchenware, restaurant china, and pottery.

Ladybug's Antiques and Collectibles
P.O. Box 574
Crystal City, MO 63019
www.tias.com/stores/lbac/
Selling a selection of glassware and pottery, with an emphasis on American pieces.

Once Upon a Table
30 Crofut Street
Pittsfield, MA 01201
413-443-6622
Owner: Carol Levison
www.onceuponatable.com
European and American period kitchenware; jadeite, bakelite, FireKing, biscuit bins, and more.

Restoration Hardware
935 Broadway
New York, NY 10011
212-260-9479
www.restorationhardware.com
Not just hardware, also home furnishings, lighting and home and garden accessories.

Ruby Beets Antiques
Poxybogue Road
Bridgehampton, NY 11932
516-537-2802
Antique painted furniture, old china, and kitchenware.

Sotheby's
1334 York Avenue at 72nd Street
New York, NY 10021
212-606-7000
www.sothebys.com
Public auctions.

Tri-State Antique Center
47 West Pike
Canonsburg, PA 15317
724-745-9116
http://tristateantiques.com
Specializes in Heywood-Wakefield, Mid-Century Modern furniture, and pottery, china, and glass.

Up The Creek's
American Antique Furniture Market
120 South Tower
Centralia, WA 98531
360-330-0427
www.amerantfurn.com
American furniture and lighting in Victorian, Eastlake, turn-of-the-century, Mission, Arts & Crafts, Depression and 1940's Classic Revival periods in both restored and original finish.

Victor DiPaola Antiques
Long Island, NY
516-488-5868
www.dipaolaantiques.com
Furniture and decorative arts of the 18th and 19th centuries.

A listing of over 40,000 antiques shops throughout the country exists at www.curioscape.com.

DISPLAY CASES

Collector's Display Case Company
512 North Spruce Street
Valley, NE 68064-9670
402-359-5539
www.mb3.net/display/
Offers unique, clear lightweight plastic display cases for every type of collectible. Also dish displays, showcases, domes, and much more.

Indian River Display Case Company
13706 Robins Road
Westerville, OH 43082
800-444-1280
http://members.aol.com/JanieW48/index.html
Sells both hardwood and metal display frame cases in many shapes and sizes.

Hold Everything
1309–1311 Second Avenue
New York, NY 10021
212-879-1450
www.williamssonoma.com/brands/brands.clm
Mainstream provider for everything for storage and display, from baskets to bookshelves.

Scottco Products Inc.
5529 Dial Drive
P.O. Box 8015
Granite City, IL 62040
800-238-4540
www.scottcoproducts.com
Collector display cases for any paper items. Solid oak framing with museum quality non-glare uv windows, hanging slots and support stands for wall or table display.

FLEA MARKETS

Alameda Swap Meet
Located on South Alameda Blvd.
Los Angeles, CA 90021
213-233-2764
Well-known, wide selection; held 7 days a week from 10 a.m. to 7 p.m. year round, 400 vendors.

Aunt Tinker's General Store
Highway 19
Big Spring, MO 63363
573-252-4707
Known for its unusual collectibles, this market is open daily from 10 a.m. to 5 p.m.

Brimfield Antique Show
Route 20
Brimfield, MA 01010
413-245-3436
www.brimfieldshow.com
Renowned as the Outdoor Antiques Capital of the World, this show is held for a week in the months of May, July, and September.

Denver Indoor Antique Market
1212 South Broadway
Denver, CO 80210
303-744-7049
Open seven days a week.

Merriam Lane Flea Market
14th and Merriam Lane
Kansas City, KS 66106
913-677-0833
Open air market where Estates are bought and sold; operates weekly in Spring and Summer from 7 a.m. to dark.

Ruth's Flea Market
Highway 431
Roanoke, AL 36274
334-864-7328
Over 300 booths selling all types of collectibles, new and old; weekly on Wednesdays and Saturdays.

Sullivan Flea Market
Heights Ravenna Road
5 Miles West of Ravenna Center
Ravenna, MI 49451
616-853-2435
Antiques, collectibles, fresh produce, and consignment; weekly on Mondays from April to the end of October.

Tesuque Pueblo Flea Market
Route 5
Santa Fe, NM 87501
505-660-8948
Native American Crafts, antiques, rugs, collectibles, and southwest furniture, both new and used; monthly Friday to Sunday. Call to verify specific dates.

Traders Village (Houston)
Eldridge Road
Houston, TX 77083
713-890-5500
Largest market on the Texas Gulf Coast, with over 800 dealers; Saturday & Sunday, 8 a.m. to 6 p.m, year-round.

Vintage Village
I-77 and U.S. Highway
Hamptonville, NC 27020
910-468-8616
New and old collectibles; Fridays 10 a.m–4 p.m., and Saturday and Sunday 8 a.m. to 5 p.m.

For listings of flea markets held throughout the country, go to www.fleamarketguide.com.

MODERN PIECES

Anthropologie
375 West Broadway
New York, NY
800 309 2500 for your nearest store
www.anthropologie.com
Furniture and home furnishings.

B & B Italia USA
150 East 58th Street
New York, NY 10155
800-872-1697
www.bebitalia.it
Modern furniture.

Cassina USA Inc.
155 East 56th Street
New York, NY 10022
800-770-3568
www.CassinaUSA.com
Furniture by Mackintosh, Le Corbusier, Rietveld, Frank Lloyd Wright and more.

Crate & Barrel
646 N Michigan Avenue
Chicago, IL 60611
800-996-9960
www.crateandbarrel.com
Good-value furniture and accessories.

Design Within Reach
455 Jackson Street
San Francisco, CA 94111
800-944-2233
www.dwr.com
Furniture from over fifty designers including Alessi, Gehry, and Knoll.

Domus Design Collection
181 Madison Avenue
New York, NY 10016
212-685-0800
www.ddcnyc.com
Modern designs by Pralo, Mari, Dordoni, and many others.

Full Upright Position
1101 NW Glisan
Portland, OR 97209
800-431-5134
www.fup.com
Furniture by Aalto, Eames, Le Corbusier, van der Rohe and more.

Gansevoort Gallery
72 Gansevoort Street
New York, NY 10014
212-633-0555
www.gansevoortgallery.com
Contemporary pieces in metal, lighting, glass, furniture, wood, and ceramics.

Heywood-Wakefield Company
2300 SW 23rd Street
Miami, FL 33145
305-858-4240
www.heywood-wakefield.com
Modern and vintage pieces and fabric selections.

Ikea
1800 East McConnor Parkway
Schaumburg, IL 60173
800-434-4532
www.ikea.com
Home basics at great prices.

John Widdicomb
560 Fifth Street NW
Grand Rapids, MI 49504-5208
800-847-9433
www.johnwiddicomb.com
Exclusively designed furniture by the original maker.

Knoll
1235 Water Street
East Greenville, PA 18041
877-61-KNOLL
www.knoll.com
Producers of modern furniture by modern architects since 1938.

Louis Poulsen Lighting
3260 Meridian Parkway
Ft. Lauderdale, FL 33331
954-349-2525
www.louispoulsen.com
Exclusive collection of tabletop, ceiling, table, and floor lighting fixtures.

Modernica
2118 East Seventh Place
Los Angeles, CA 90021
800-665-3839
www.modernica.net
Seating, tables, lighting, and modular shelving from mid-century designers.

MOMA Design Store
44 West 53rd Street
New York, NY 10022
800-447-6662
www.momastore.org
Furniture and accessories by modern designers such as Stark and Vasa.

O Group (Eva Zeisel Designs)
152 Franklin Street
New York, NY 10013
212-431-5973
www.theorangechicken.com
Deals exclusively in Eva Ziesel's designs.

Pastense
915 Cole Street, Suite 150
San Francisco, CA 94117-4315
415-242-0128
www.pastense.com
Classic diner furnishings, including booths, tables, chairs, and stools.

Pottery Barn
P.O. Box 7044
San Francisco
CA 94120-7044
800 922 9934 for your nearest store
www.potterybarn.com
Everything from furniture to decoration details, such as muslin curtains, china, pillows, and candlesticks.

Retromodern.com
805 Peachtree Street
Atlanta, GA 30308
877-724-0093
www.retromodern.com
Designs for the home from Alessi, Nono, Kartell, ICF, Knoll, and more.

The Conran Shop
Bridgemarket
415 East 59th Street
New York, NY 10022
212-755-9079
Modern home furnishings, kitchenware, tableware, and bathroom accessories.

Vitra Design Museum
204 Pennsylvania Avenue, Suite B
Easton, MD 21601
410-763-7698
www.vitra.com
Designs for the home from Gehry, Thiel, Nelson, Eames, and others.

picture credits

Key: t = top, b = below, l = left, r = right, c = center

Front & back endpapers: Elena Colombo's apartment in New York; **1** Jonathan Adler & Simon Doonan's apartment in New York; **2** Laura Stoddart's apartment in London; **3** VV Rouleaux ribbons, trimmings & braids; **5 & 6** Martin Barrell & Amanda Sellers' flat, owners of Maisonette, London; **7** Lulu Guinness's home in London; **8-9** Designer Ann-Louise Roswald's apartment in London; **10 l** Artist Hunt Slonem's own loft in New York; **11 tr** Elena Colombo's apartment in New York; **11bl & br** Laura Stoddart's apartment in London; **12 &13** Lulu Guinness's home in London; **14 l** A New York city apartment designed by Marino & Giolito; **14 r** Jonathan Adler & Simon Doonan's apartment in New York; **15 l** Architect François Muracciole's apartment in Paris; **15 r** Lesley Dilcock's house in London; **16 l** BDDW retail showroom, New York **16 r** Lulu Guinness's home in London; **17** Lesley Dilcock's house in London; **17 b** Josephine Ryan Antiques; **18** Lesley Dilcock's house in London; **19 tr** Lulu Guinness's home in London; **19 bl** VV Rouleaux ribbons, trimmings & braids; **19br** Martin Barrell & Amanda Sellers' flat, owners of Maisonette, London; **20 tl** Lesley Dilcock's house in London; **20 bl** Lulu Guinness's home in London; **20 br** Laura Stoddart's apartment in London; **21, 22 l & 22-23c** Martin Barrell & Amanda Sellers' flat, owners of Maisonette, London; **23 r** Kimberley Watson's house in London; **24** Designer Ann-Louise Roswald's apartment in London; **25 l & r** VV Rouleaux ribbons, trimmings & braids; **25 c** Lulu Guinness's home in London; **26 & 27 tr** Martin Barrell & Amanda Sellers' flat, owners of Maisonette, London; **27 br** Laura Stoddart's apartment in London; **28 l** Architect François Muracciole's apartment in Paris; **28 tr & br** Photographer Marie-Pierre Morel's house in Paris, designed by François Muracciole; **29** VV Rouleaux ribbons, trimmings & braids; **30 & 31 l** Kimberley Watson's house in London; **32 l & 33** Lulu Guinness's home in London; **34 & 35** Elena Colombo's apartment in New York; **36 tl & bl** Interior designer and owner of Immaculate House Tatyana Hill's apartment in London; **36-37** Architect François Muracciole's apartment in Paris; **37 r** Photographer Marie-Pierre Morel's house in Paris, designed by François Muracciole; **38-41** Lesley Dilcock's house in London; **42 tl** Jonathan Adler & Simon Doonan's apartment in New York; **42 bl & 42-43 c** Kari Sigerson's apartment in New York; **43 r** Renée Snyder, New York; **44** Gallery & bookshop owner Françoise de Nobele's apartment in Paris ; **45** Lulu Guinness's home in London; **46 & 47** Lesley Dilcock's house in London; **48 & 49** Sean & Mary Kelly's loft in New York, designed by Steven Learner, all art courtesy of Sean Kelly Gallery, New York; **48 l** mirror by Douglas Gordon "Retrace your steps/Remember tomorrow" 1999, vinyl, text and mirror; reflected in mirror: upper row Ann Hamilton "untitled" (body object series), bottom row Douglas Gordon "Psycho Hitchhiker" 1993; back wall Anthony Gormley "untitled" 1986-87; **48r** far left Jannis Kounellis "untitled" 1978 pencil and charcoal on paper; second from left Joseph Beuys "untitled" 1948 graphite on paper; center left Louise Bourgeois "untitled" 1947 ink on paper; center right Marcel Duchamp "Bec Aver" 1965 etching on japon paper; third from right Juliâo Sarmento "5 Elementos" 1974, 2 black and white polaroids; second from right Man Ray "Le Dernier Oeuvre de Duchamp" 1968, vintage black and white photograph; right Douglas Gordon "Psycho Hitchhiker" 1993, black and white photograph; **49** far left wall Ann Hamilton "untitled" (body object series), 1987, 1991; black and white photographs in artist-designed frames; far right Lorna Simpson "Twenty Questions (A Sampler)" 1986, 4 circular silver gelatin prints, 6 engraved plastic plaques; **50** Lesley Dilcock's house in London; **51 l** Renée Snyder, New York; **51 r** A New York city apartment designed by Marino & Giolito; **52 & 53** Artist Hunt Slonem's own loft in New York; **54-55** Designer Ann-Louise Roswald's apartment in London; **56 t** Elena Colombo's apartment in New York; **56 b & 57** Designer Ann-Louise Roswald's apartment in London; **58** Martin Barrell & Amanda Sellers' flat, owners of Maisonette, London; **59** Laura Stoddart's apartment in London;

ARCHITECTS & DESIGNERS WHOSE WORK IS FEATURED IN THIS BOOK:

Key: t = top, b = below, l = left,
r = right, c = center

Jonathan Adler
465 Broome Street
New York, NY 10013
USA
t. 212 941 8950
Pages 1, 42tl, 105bc, 110

BDDW
Design/Build Furniture,
Furnishings & Architecture
8 Rivington Street
New York, NY 10002
USA
t. 212 673 5111
f. 212 673 5050

e. info@bddw.com
www.bddw.com
Pages 84r, 88bl & br, 161

Elena Colombo
Sculptor and designer
e. eacolombo@earthlink.net
Front & back endpapers and pages 11tr, 34 & 35, 56t, 85t, 85b, 86-87bc, 88t, 104, 108 & 109tr

Lulu Guinness
3 Ellis Street
London SW1X 9AL
t. + 44 20 7823 4828
f. + 44 20 7823 4889
www.luluguinness.com
Pages 7, 12 & 13, 16r, 19tr, 20bl, 25c, 32l & 33, 45, 60l, 86-87tc & 87t, 116, 121r

Immaculate House
Locations in Mayfair and Spitalfields
Mayfair (flagship store):
4 & 5 Burlington Arcade
London W1J 0PD
t. + 44 20 7499 5758
f. + 44 20 7493 5852
e. tvaldabhil@aol.com
Spitalfields (furniture and outlet)
57-59 Brushfield Street
London E1 6AA
t. + 44 20 7375 1844
f. + 44 20 7375 1886
e. tvaldabhil@aol.com
Pages 36tl & bl, 65b, 68tl & 68-69, 87b, 92l

Sean Kelly Gallery
528 West 29th Street
New York, NY 10001
USA
t. 212 239 1181
f. 212 239 2467
www.skny.com
Pages 48 & 49, 75br, 80-81

Maisonette
79 Chamberlayne Road
London NW10 3ND
t. + 44 20 8964 8444
f. + 44 20 8964 8464
e. maisonetteUK@aol.com
Pages 5 & 6, 19br, 21, 22l & 22-23c, 26 & 27 tr, 58, 70, 113b, 127

60 l Lulu Guinness's home in London; 60 r & 61 Artist Hunt Slonem's own loft in New York; 62, 63 l & 63 r Gallery & bookshop owner Françoise de Nobele's apartment in Paris; 63 c Architect François Muracciole's apartment in Paris; 64 l Kimberley Watson's house in London; 64-65 Laura Stoddart's apartment in London; 65 t Kimberley Watson's house in London; 65 b Interior designer and owner of Immaculate House Tatyana Hill's apartment in London; 66, 67 t & bl Laura Stoddart's apartment in London; 67 br Kimberley Watson's house in London; 68 tl & 68-69 c Interior designer and owner of Immaculate House Tatyana Hill's apartment in London; 68 bl Laura Stoddart's apartment in London ; 69 r Lesley Dilcock's house in London; 70 Martin Barrell & Amanda Sellers' flat, owners of Maisonette, London; 71, 72 & 73 Kimberley Watson's house in London; 74 & 75 tl Laura Stoddart's apartment in London; 75 br Sean & Mary Kelly's loft in New York, designed by Steven Learner, art courtesy of Sean Kelly Gallery, New York, Joseph Kosuth "Ithaca Circle" 2000, warm white neon; 77 l Photographer Marie-Pierre Morel's house in Paris, designed by François Muracciole; 77 br Kari Sigerson's apartment in New York; 78 l Architect François Muracciole's apartment in Paris; 79 c & r Gallery & bookshop owner Françoise de Nobele's apartment in Paris ; 80-81 Sean & Mary Kelly's loft in New York, designed by Steven Learner, all art courtesy of Sean Kelly Gallery, New York, hanging far left Lorna Simpson "Interior/Exterior, Full/Empty # 10" 1997; center Lorna Simpson "Interior/Exterior, Full/Empty # 1" 1997; right Lorna Simpson "Twenty Questions (A Sampler)" 1986; 82-83 Kimberley Watson's house in London; 84 l Renée Snyder, New York ; 84 r BDDW retail showroom, New York; 85 t Elena Colombo's apartment in New York, painting by Lisa Stefanelli; 85 b Elena Colombo's apartment in New York; 86 t Artist Hunt Slonem's own loft in New York; 86 b Josephine Ryan Antiques ; 86-87 bc Elena Colombo's apartment in New York; 86-87 tc & 87 t Lulu Guinness's home in London; 87 b Interior designer and owner of Immaculate House Tatyana Hill's apartment in London; 88 t Elena Colombo's apartment in New York; 88 bl & br BDDW retail showroom, New York; 89 t Photographer Marie-Pierre Morel's house in Paris, designed by François Muracciole; 89 b Interior designer and owner of Immaculate House Tatyana Hill's apartment in London; 90 tl Renée Snyder; 90 bl Lesley Dilcock's house in London; 90 br Photographer Marie-Pierre Morel's house in Paris, designed by François Muracciole; 91 Artist Hunt Slonem's own loft in New York; 92 l Interior designer and owner of Immaculate House Tatyana Hill's apartment in London; 92 c Kimberley Watson's house in London; 92 r A New York city apartment designed by Marino & Giolito; 93 Gallery & bookshop owner Françoise de Nobele's apartment in Paris; 94 l Kimberley Watson's house in London; 95 r Photographer Marie-Pierre Morel's house in Paris, designed by François Muracciole; 97 l VV Rouleaux ribbons, trimmings & braids; 98 l Gallery & bookshop owner Françoise de Nobele's apartment in Paris ; 98 r Kari Sigerson's apartment in New York; 99 VV Rouleaux ribbons, trimmings & braids ; 100 l Photographer Marie-Pierre Morel's house in Paris, designed by François Muracciole; 100 tr Laura Stoddart's apartment in London; 100 br Kari Sigerson's apartment in New York; 101 l Renée Snyder, New York ; 101 r A New York city apartment designed by Marino & Giolito; 102 Photographer Marie-Pierre Morel's house in Paris, designed by François Muracciole; 103 l A New York city apartment designed by Marino & Giolito; 103 r Kari Sigerson's apartment in New York; 104 Elena Colombo's apartment in New York; 105 l Renée Snyder, New York ; 105 tr Architect François Muracciole's apartment in Paris; 105 bc Jonathan Adler & Simon Doonan's apartment in New York; 106 tl & 106-107 c VV Rouleaux ribbons, trimmings & braids; 107 r Artist Hunt Slonem's own loft in New York; 108 & 109 tr Elena Colombo's apartment in New York; 109 b Architect François Muracciole's apartment in Paris; 110 Jonathan Adler & Simon Doonan's apartment in New York; 112 & 113 tr Kimberley Watson's house in London; 113 b Martin Barrell & Amanda Sellers' flat, owners of Maisonette, London; 116 Lulu Guinness's home in London; 117 Kimberley Watson's house in London; 118 r A New York city apartment designed by Marino & Giolito; 119 Architect François Muracciole's apartment in Paris; 120-121 Kimberley Watson's house in London; 121 r Lulu Guinness's home in London; 127 Martin Barrell & Amanda Sellers' flat, owners of Maisonette, London.

Marino & Giolito
Architecture/Interior Design
161 West 16th Street
New York, NY 10011
USA
t. 212 675 5737
f. 212 675 5737
e. marino.giolito@rcn.com
Pages 14l, 51r, 92r, 101r, 103l, 118r

François Muracciole
Architecture & Design
House, Office, Shops, Furniture & More
54 rue de Montreuil
75011 Paris
France
t. +33 1 43 71 33 03
f. +33 1 43 71 20 50
e. françois.muracciole@libertysurf.fr
Pages 15l, 28l, 36-37, 63c, 78l, 105tr, 109b, 119

Françoise de Nobele Antiquitès
2, rue de Bourbon le Chateau
75006 Paris
France
Pages 44, 62, 63l & 63r, 79c & r, 93, 98l

Ann-Louise Roswald Ltd
Fashion, textiles & interior design
Top Floor Studio
7 Corsham Street
London N1 6DP
t. + 44 20 7250 1583
f. + 44 20 7684 8790
e. ann-louise@annlouiseroswald.com
www.annlouiseroswald.com
Pages 8-9, 24, 54-55, 56b & 57

Josephine Ryan Antiques
63 Abbeville Road
London SW4 9JW
t. + 44 20 8675 3900
Pages 17b, 86b

Hunt Slonem
Artist
Represented by:
Marlborough Gallery NYC
40 West 57th Street
New York, NY 10019
USA
t. 212 541 4900
Pages 10l, 52 & 53, 60r & 61, 86t, 91, 107r

VV Rouleaux Atelier
Furniture at Harrods
54 Sloane Square
London SW1W 8AX
t. + 44 20 7730 3125
f. + 44 20 7730 9985
e. design@vvrouleaux.com
www.vvrouleaux.com

VV Rouleaux
Ribbons, trimmings & braids
6 Marylebone High Street
London W1U 4NJ
t. + 44 20 7224 5179
f. + 44 20 7224 5193
e. design@vvrouleaux.com
www.vvrouleaux.com
Pages 3, 19bl, 25l & r, 29, 97l, 99, 106tl & 106-107c

index

Figures in italics indicate captions.

Acknowledgments

An enormous thank you to Catherine, whose photographic talent just keeps on growing, resulting in the fabulous pictures for this book. Thanks, too, for being such a good friend and great fun to work with. Penny Tattersall remains the best agent in the business and deserves an award for steering Catherine and me through this book while working on her own production—baby Millie! To Stuart, many thanks for unveiling the mysteries of the computer to the totally ignorant. For Barbara, a big hug for helping out as always, and to Hannah, lots of love and thanks for holding the fort. To those who were part of the project at Ryland Peters & Small, a big thank you, especially to Annabel, who had to make sense of my ramblings. I am greatly indebted to those who let us into their homes and workspaces with such good grace. Love to my family and friends for their interest and support. And to Letty, my daughter, hugs and kisses for being so cooperative and enthusiastic.